Towns and Cities

EMRYS JONES

Towns and Cities

OXFORD UNIVERSITY PRESS
London   Oxford   New York

Oxford University Press

LONDON OXFORD GLASGOW NEW YORK
TORONTO MELBOURNE WELLINGTON CAPE TOWN
IBADAN NAIROBI DAR ES SALAAM LUSAKA ADDIS ABABA
KUALA LUMPUR SINGAPORE JAKARTA HONG KONG TOKYO
DELHI BOMBAY CALCUTTA MADRAS KARACHI

ISBN 0 19 888013 8

© OXFORD UNIVERSITY PRESS 1966

First published as an Oxford University Press paperback 1966
Sixth impression 1976

All rights reserved. No part of this publication may be reproduced, stored in a retrieval system, or transmitted, in any form or by any means, electronic, mechanical, photocopying, recording or otherwise, without the prior permission of Oxford University Press

This book is sold subject to the condition that it shall not, by way of trade or otherwise, be lent, re-sold, hired out, or otherwise circulated without the publisher's prior consent in any form of binding or cover other than that in which it is published and without a similar condition including this condition being imposed on the subsequent purchaser.

PRINTED AND BOUND IN ENGLAND BY
HAZELL WATSON AND VINEY LTD, AYLESBURY, BUCKS

Contents

1	What is a Town?	1
2	The Process of Urbanization	13
3	Pre-Industrial Cities	38
4	The Western City	52
5	Size and Classification of Cities	80
6	The City and the Region	93
7	Man and the City	104
	Bibliography	143
	Index	146

Illustrations

Fig.

1. Percentage of population living in towns of over 20,000 inhabitants by countries — 15
2. Pre-industrial cities: (a) Oyo (Nigeria); (b) Nazirabad (India); (c) Chungking (China) — 41
3. Pre-industrial cities: (a) Peking (China); (b) Petare (Venezuela); (c) Caracas (Venezuela) — 47
4. Edinburgh: the medieval centre and 18th-century additions — 53
5. The industrial city: (a) 19th-century English town; (b) Chicago — 57
6. Layout of a neighbourhood in a new town (Hemel Hempstead) — 68
7. City forms: (a) core; (b) radial; (c) linear; (d) ring; (e) dispersed; (f) dispersed with nodes — 70
8. Areas of specialized functions in Central London — 76
9. Christaller's hexagonal hierarchy of regions — 86
10. The city regions of France — 87
11. Regions of influence: (a) market town criteria (Wales); (b) local bus service regions (Cornwall); (c) London regions — 98
12. Age/sex differences within a city (Belfast) — 118
13. Negro segregation: (a) New York; (b) Chicago — 126

Fig.		
14	Religious segregation (Belfast)	132
15	Zone of old and condemned houses (Belfast)	136
16	The growth of slum areas (Belfast)	137
17	Burgess's diagram of city ecology	139

Acknowledgements

Fig. 10 is taken from J. Carrière, *Le Fait urbain en France*, Paris, 1964, p. 74.

Figs. 2a, b, and c, 5a and b, and 17 are taken from E. Jones, *Human Geography*, Chatto and Windus, London, 1964.

Figs. 12, 14, 15, and 16 are taken from E. Jones, *A Social Geography of Belfast*, Oxford University Press, London, 1961.

1
What is a Town?

(i)

THERE CAN BE few human institutions which have evoked such depth of feeling and contradictory attitudes as the city. On the one hand it has been equated with the height of man's achievement. The Latin root is shared with the word 'civilization', suggesting that outside the orbit of the city is the uncivilized, the uncouth, the barbaric; inside flowered the great cultures of human history. Here technical skill achieved its utmost, schools of thought flourished, and the arts prospered and the human spirit was raised to its highest pinnacles. On the other hand the growth of the city—and in particular of the industrial city of the nineteenth century—brought its own retribution. The city was a consumer of mankind, for until recently no city grew by its own natural increase; it fed on those who lived beyond it but could not resist its lure; it offered disease and misery, poverty and want to millions; at its worst it made human life cheap and human values worthless. There is a City of God and there is a Babylon, and these are both the same city. But many are blind to one or the other. To Rousseau, 'Cities are the final pit of the human spirit.' Shelley would have agreed: 'Hell is a city just like London.' Yet, in Johnson's view, 'When a man is tired of London, he is tired of life.'

It is not strange, therefore, that the city, which has excited such extreme reactions, has attracted the student; that there are so many books, so many theories and viewpoints, which seek to describe, explain, analyse, praise, and denigrate. In the last few decades, when it seems as if we may indeed be overwhelmed by the city, increasing efforts have been made to understand its origins and growth, the reasons for its birth, how it functions, what are its effects, to what extent it controls or is controlled by society. The increasing urgency is due not only to the degree to which so-called Western societies have become urbanized, by the growth in north-west Europe and North America of the super-city, the megalopolis, a many-headed giant which dwarfs all pre-existing ideas of the city. But even greater urgency is called for to meet the newer, no less startling, and possibly even more rapid urbanization which is now characterizing Latin America and, to a lesser extent, Asia. Here peasants become city-dwellers overnight. In the last decade the number of 'million' cities in the tropics has risen from four to fourteen; and whereas major European cities are not increasing as phenomenally as they did during the last century, major tropical cities are growing by leaps and bounds. Saigon has increased by nearly sixteen times in twenty years. Yet we still know very little about the city, even about our own cities which have so long a tradition.

The English are a nation of town- and city-dwellers. However much an Englishman may delight in his rural heritage, boast of the village pump, dream of a green and pleasant land, his everyday world is the city street, his meeting-place the market square, and his reality is Jerusalem, however sadly fallen from the ideal. There is, of course, an extreme reluctance to recognize the fact. No one has done more than the Englishman to bring the country into the town. *Rus in urbe*—perhaps his most distinctive contribution to town planning—has given us delightful green squares, contrasting greatly with their paved continental counterparts. It has given us garden suburbs, and probably contributed most to the uniqueness of which Rasmussen wrote so eloquently in his book on London. Unfortunately it has also meant suburbs which have compromised the countryside with a travesty of the town. This unwillingness to accept the town derives from the ambivalent attitude already referred to. If one distinguishes as clearly as the English between country and town, then the latter is a very poor second. God, after all, made the first, and man the second. We are still extremely jealous of our countryside—probably because four out of five Englishmen live in towns—but our problems are urban ones. They are the nearly intolerable problems of city growth and decay, of congestion and commuting, of traffic and communications. Within a matter of weeks in early 1963 three important reports appeared, the first on traffic in towns, the second on the growth of London and the south-east, the third on the possibilities of relocating offices outside London. They did little more than underline the size of the problems. More than ever the need for trying to understand the city and how it works has become urgent. Strange though it may seem, we may have overcome the evils which we associate with the industrial squalor of the last century only to make way for other evils. Our cities are healthier than ever, problems of waste disposal, sanitation, and water supply are easily overcome, and pollution is being controlled, but as a result town populations are generating themselves: concentrations of humanity are reaching unprecedented degrees; new diseases appear—results of the frustration of long journeys to work, of fatigue. The perfecting of the institution may be bringing about its own destruction. The attraction is balanced by a retreat from the city. The centre becomes empty and meaningless at night, but not perhaps as meaningless as the retreats themselves—the million tiny villas which make up our suburbs.

How can one best approach the study of so complex a phenomenon, at once so familiar and yet so difficult to understand? In the very first place, how best can we define it? Strange though it may seem, the city defies a universal definition which would be acceptable to everyone. Is it a physical conglomeration of streets and houses, or is it a centre of exchange and commerce? Or is it a kind of society, or even a frame of mind? Has it a certain size, a specific density? The difficulties involved in definition are countless, and there is very little unanimity: it seems to be all things to all men.

Every country has to have a definition of towns and cities for census purposes, and a glance at some of these will illustrate the variety of definitions. Some countries adopt a simple numerical value. A town or city is bigger than a village community, and if we are dealing with very large settlements there is often little doubt. But at the lower end of the scale, if size is the criterion, who is to say what the size of a town is? In Denmark a settlement of 200 people constitutes a town, as it does in Sweden and Finland. In Greece a settlement must have over 10,000 inhabitants before it can be called a town. Between these is a great variety of figures. A thousand inhabitants makes a town in Canada, but 2,500 in the United States. A thousand is enough in Venezuela, but there must be 5,000 people to make a town in Ghana. Clearly numbers alone mean very little. There are circumstances in which a numerically small settlement may have urban characteristics—like density, markets, administrative functions—and others in which a numerically large settlement may be a specialized research station, like Harwell, or is still obviously a village in which the vast majority of men are farmers. The latter is certainly the case in agricultural states and in the developing countries. In India, for example, it is specified that to be a town a settlement must not only have more than 5,000 inhabitants, but its density must be over 1,000 to a square mile, and over 75% of its adult male population must be engaged in work other than agriculture.

This last definition suggests other criteria, namely density and function. We certainly think of most cities as being densely populated, though this need not be universally true. But with the exception of India, density is rarely used as a criterion. More critical than density is function, for it is generally accepted that one of the distinguishing characteristics of a town or city is the fact that its work is divorced from the soil: its people are not primarily food-producers. Yet very few states include function in the definition, partly because it is implied in most as an urban characteristic. India, as we have seen, defines this function accurately. Israel refuses the status of a town to settlements of over 2,000 if more than a third of the heads of households are engaged in agriculture; and the Congo accepts the figure of 2,000 with the proviso that they must be predominantly non-agricultural.

The administrative function of a town is most clearly brought out by those states who use this as a sole criterion. This is so in Turkey, Czechoslovakia, the Dominican Republic, and the United Arab Republic. Many more define their towns by giving them a certain kind of government, as in Algeria, Japan, Tunisia, and, most familiar, the United Kingdom. This really means that the city or town is so by definition—a town is what the state is prepared to call a town. This does not help us very much. It is even more frustrating when a solecism is introduced as in Rumania, where a town is a settlement having urban characteristics. The wheel has come full circle. As one writer put it despairingly, 'A city is a city is a city.'

Reference is continually made to towns and cities. What is the difference? Taking the line of least resistance we could say that a city is a town which has been designated a city. This would be true in many states, including the United Kingdom, but it would confuse as much as it enlightens. In Britain we commonly associate a city with a cathedral, and historically there may be justification for this. But one could never think of St. Asaph, for example, as a city; and the distinction is one which is normally granted under specific circumstances. Yet there are historians of the city who recognize the distinction as being real and significant. Pirenne, in his study of the medieval city, did not deny many urban attributes to towns, but he reserved the full accolade of city to those whose economic functions were of a high level. Certainly if one recognizes degrees of urban-ness, those who qualify at the lower end—functionally

WHAT IS A TOWN?

towns because they are non-agricultural and have a considerable population at high density—may be very different from those at the upper end, where the non-material aspects of civilization, together with their manifestation in institutions and monumental architecture, seem to imply a different level of existence. Where this becomes relevant attention will be drawn to it, but otherwise the emphasis will be on characteristics common to both, and the words 'town' or 'city' may be used interchangeably to avoid resort to the clumsy phrase 'urban settlement'.

One last point on legal definitions. They vary so much that the common denominator—which is one of the things we must look for—may seem non-existent, in which case comparative studies of urbanization appear impossible. In fact the simple numerical index can be used on a world scale if enough allowance is made to clear possible contradictions among small settlements. Above 5,000 people there is less doubt that we are dealing with something urban, above 10,000 hardly any doubt at all. The recommendation of the U.N. on grading agglomerations by size is acceptable where the population is above 5,000. The difficulties arise at the point where a village is almost a town, or a town nearly indistinguishable from a village. At that point it is better to accept the local definition. A town is what is implied by the local people when they call a locality a town. If this differs from the criterion we use for statistical analysis it is no less real. It may be much more meaningful than all the scholarly efforts at defining something too rich and varied to be caught by statistics. The latter have their uses, but it would be a pity if the humanity of cities were destroyed by academic niceties. Defining a town, whether in economic or legal terms or merely by size, does not take us very much further towards understanding the nature of urbanism. It merely suggests some of the concomitants of urbanism without telling us which are universal or which are important. Is there a common factor, and if so, does it lie in the form of a city, or in its function, or in its society? There are almost as many answers to these questions as there are students interested in cities.

(ii)

In the first place it should be understood that we are looking for universals, for common elements, shared manifestations. There is a sense, of course, in which every city is unique, a discrete entity occupying a unique position and having a unique history. Many historical studies of individual towns have used this approach, sometimes isolating a particular one from the very context which explains it. The concern with individual cities is put very strongly in Asa Briggs's recent book on Victorian cities, in which he states that the historian 'will find that his most interesting task is to show in what respect cities differ from each other'. This is a legitimate point of view, but it would tell us little about cities in general. There was only one Athens, there is only one London, but in a study of cities and of urbanization the accent must be on the Greek city state and on the modern industrial metropolis. The unique must be subservient to the general.

The historical approach has by no means been confined to or even mainly concerned with studies of individual cities. But those studies concerned with the nature and origin of cities in general have tended to see the entire explanation in terms of one exclusive set of factors. To Pirenne all the facets of city life in medieval times, when the European city was established, could be explained in economic terms. To him the city was a community of merchants. The force of his classic work lay in the skilful development of this simple central thesis. He traced the growth of commerce in early medieval Europe and the way in which certain settlements responded—largely because of their favoured location. Contact between Venice and the eastern world centring on Constantinople gave rise to the great entrepreneur cities of Lombardy; contact between northern Europe and Scandinavia and Russia centred on the Netherlands. Elsewhere in Europe great fairs were established where peripatetic merchants met to exchange goods. These were usually at already existing settlements. Pirenne distinguished sharply between the existing towns and the cities into which some of these towns grew. The towns had their own markets, but these were strictly local and therefore in a different category from the few centres which served as economic foci for the whole of Europe. The latter became cities. Sometimes economic locational advantages were enough, and cities arose where there had been no privileged market previously. 'Geographical advantage plus the presence of a town or a fortified burgh seems the essential and necessary condition for a colony of merchants.' What Pirenne envisaged was a Europe of small market towns—none with more than a strictly local significance—which witnessed a commercial renaissance in the 10th century. This transformed some of them into cities which were consequently distinguished by merchant and manufacturing classes, and eventually by a middle class, all organized within a set of new communal institutions. The town was a stepping-stone to the city.

Few writers have given such primacy to the commercial function. Some classic contributions have stressed other facets. The importance of legal institutions came first for H. S. Maine and F. W. Maitland. Again, put in its simplest terms, this meant that the distinction between a borough and a village lay mainly in its organization: the former was a corporate body and the latter was not. Other institutional theories have given religion a central place in explaining the origin of towns.

The weakness of most of these theories is that they are too exclusive. It is true that Pirenne, for example, recognized factors other than the economic—such as the need for defence and the rise of crafts and manufacturing—but he relegated these to a very secondary order. In doing so he probably weakened his thesis. None of the single explanations is a sufficient condition of a city, though it may be a necessary condition.

An interesting development and expansion of the idea of the city as crossroads has been made by Robert S. Lopez.[1] He takes as a symbol of the city the earliest known ideogram, an Egyptian hieroglyph. This is a cross within a circle, and to Lopez this symbolizes the city's origin and function. The cross stands for convergence, the meeting, not only of merchandise, but of men and ideas. The circle stands for the moat or wall, but although this is historically so often the case it may further symbolize the compactness of a community, or even the moral barriers it can erect to protect its society. This ideogram is the oldest 'definition' of a city, says Lopez, and the most fitting. He summarizes it in the words 'communication plus togetherness'. The interest of this theory lies in its suggestions and explanations not only of origins and growth, but also of possible decline. With growing speed of transport the convergence could become—as indeed it has in the modern city—a handicap: the centre may lose the main thing it once offered—accessibility. In the same way the function of a wall can change from protection to confinement: it can be a hindrance to growth; it can symbolize the cutting off of a city from the outside world, and this could lead to decline. Lopez suggests that Pirenne was satisfied with the crossroads symbol, and that this was not enough. In adding the circle he has introduced a wider concept. One could still criticize the symbolism. It has been said that the cross is too exclusive a symbol, and that it could well have been a mason's hammer—i.e., the symbol of industrialization rather than convergence.

[1] R. S. Lopez, 'The Crossroads within the Wall' in O. Handlin and J. Burchard (eds.), *The Historian and the City*, Cambridge, Mass., 1963.

Even though the symbol of circle and cross may stand for the non-material aspects of urban life, Lopez's interpretation is still basically concerned with the city in a physical sense, and its function. But one can approach the city from an entirely different aspect, as many sociologists and psychologists have done. It is quite a jump from the idea of crossroads and wall to the statement that 'the city is a state of mind, a body of customs and tradition'. The concern here is with the mode of life which is thought to be characteristic of groups in a city and different from that outside the city. This is exemplified in an article by Louis Wirth called 'Urbanism as a Way of Life'.[1] His acceptance of the criteria of size and density is a necessary part of this thesis. His sociological definition of a city is 'a relatively large, dense, and permanent settlement of socially heterogeneous individuals'. If we want to simplify this to the single underlying concept, this is social heterogeneity. Size contributes to the loss of personal contact and the substitution of communication by means other than face-to-face contacts, to diversity and specialization, to anonymity. Density has the effect of throwing together this diversity and encouraging and stimulating new departures in technology and ideas. Basically, under a city structure the old social framework breaks down and a new one takes its place. With the loss of primary contacts go the decline of kinship and the weakening of family ties. The allegiance which replaces them is to diverse groups which, by their very multiplicity, encourage movement. Instability becomes a norm and mobility is given a new significance. An old American song says that 'Any old place I hang my hat is home sweet home to me'. In many ways this symbolizes urban society. It is this new social framework, this new set of group relationships which typify the city, according to Wirth.

A great amount of research has been done on the sociological differences between town and country. The differences are impressive, even in vital statistics. But whether they are as clear-cut and overwhelming today in an urbanized country like our own is becoming more debatable. On the one hand perhaps kinship ties are more difficult to eradicate than was once thought, and can still be found in great cities.[2] On the other hand many of the characteristics which used to belong only to cities no longer do so exclusively. Mobility, complex occupational and class structure, intricate group allegiance—all these things are now shared by rural communities

[1] *American Journal of Sociology*, XLIV, 1938.
[2] See P. Willmott and M. D. Young, *Family and Kinship in East London*, London, 1959.

WHAT IS A TOWN?

in Western society. This is the direct outcome of increasing communication. As far as ideas and ways of life are concerned, the cross roads symbol—which implies limited routeways as well as convergence—has broken down completely. Telephone, radio, and television are making spatial differentiation less and less relevant, and there is a sense in which a small country like Britain can be thought of as being wholly urban. Even in the more literal sense of communication the city may be disintegrating and, in so doing, blurring our concepts of what is urban and what is rural.

An immediate criticism of the too exclusively sociological approach is its disregard of the more obvious features of the city—its houses and streets and public buildings and shops. Perhaps the ideas which best married bricks and mortar on the one hand and way of life on the other came from the ecological school of Chicago in the 1920s, and were first set out in the book called *The City* by R. E. Park, E. W. Burgess, and R. D. McKenzie. The term 'ecology' implies—as it does in the natural sciences—the very close relationship between population and environment. In this case the environment is man-made, and the relationship between it and society is very intricate. As a result, distinctive culture areas are found in the city. Moreover it is suggested that the city has laws of its own which direct its growth and development. A city, then, is thought to conform to a strict pattern. Part of this pattern is social, but the emphasis is on the fact that these arise inside a network of neighbourhoods and localities. 'A city represents an externally organised unit in space produced by laws of its own.' Space is given a new meaning. Not only does one now recognize distinctive parts of the city such as the slum, the industrial district, the middle-class residential district, and so on; but these are so related one to another that they set up a recognizable pattern. According to Burgess, Western towns are zoned concentrically. The ecologist sees his task as one of discovering these relationships and patterns and constructing the laws which govern them. Some of their concepts have necessarily been a little crude, but they have certainly led to research which has given new insight into the city and how it works. The main criticism which social scientists make is that the purely sociological concepts are too weak, and that the city environment is stressed at the expense of the society which gave rise to it. Others welcome the reintroduction into the picture of the fabric of the city, and the new emphasis on place and the way in which this reflects social, economic, and historical forces.

To a geographer in particular this coming down to earth is most acceptable, particularly in the awakened interest which geographers are showing in the city. Perhaps his own approach has always been the most matter of fact, because in the past it has emphasized the part played by the physical environment, particularly in the siting of cities. Sociologists like Cooley noted the significance of breaks in transportation in city origin. Vidal de la Blache[1] pointed out that this break was usually at the border of some great impediment to communication. For example a large number of cities have arisen at the foot of mountain ranges, on the fringes of great deserts like the Sahara, and of course at sea-coasts where, in particular, methods of transportation have to be changed.

The most conspicuous contributions of geographers to the study of cities do not lie in explaining sites and growth, however, but in putting the city into its regional setting. Stressing the contrast between town and country, and isolating the city as a discrete concept, in many ways falsifies the total picture beyond what is reasonable for analysis. To return to the Egyptian ideogram, the circle may lead us into the greatest error by suggesting that it also limits the roads which form the cross inside it. Commercial theories of the rise of cities, like Pirenne's, have implicit in them the extension of these roads: they are the confluence of routeways. But the focusing of attention on the 'togetherness' of the city has ignored the wider regional significance of those roads. City life is dependent on a rural area—normally the immediate countryside—for its food. It provides services for an area greatly beyond its boundaries. It is in fact a centre of exchange for a smaller or larger region around itself. Sometimes a very large city, like Constantinople at its height, depends upon—and serves—a vast area: Constantinople's wheat came from Egypt and the Black Sea, and the city dominated an Empire. Normally the relationships are more local. The Greek city state recognized this fact in deliberately ignoring the urban-rural differences as far as politics were concerned, and thus acknowledging, not the schism between two ways of life, but their interdependence.

The title of a book by R. E. Dickinson, *City and Region*, suggests the degree to which some geographers have returned to this concept. To a large extent, and particularly in an economic sense, the city reflects its region: in a complementary way the region is dependent on the city for all those specialized functions which hinge on exchange and manufacture and service. Geographers have been

---

[1] P. Vidal de la Blache, *Principles of Human Geography*, 1926 (1st English edition).

concerned not only with analysing this relationship, but with measuring it. Later chapters will deal with some of these techniques. Here it is sufficient to point out that marketing activities can easily be measured by, for example, plotting farms taking their produce to a specific market; whereas the distribution of a local newspaper will be a fair index of the spread of cultural influences from any town. What complicates the issue is that towns offer a great variety of services, from the bare minimum to the plethora offered by a city like London. This means that the index for marketing may give you one series of regions, but those for highly specialized services will give another within which are the many smaller marketing regions. There are regions within regions. This raises the point of whether there is a constant relationship between grades of regions which results in a geometric pattern. It certainly demonstrates that towns of different sizes may be arranged in a series offering different services and having different structures. A. E. Smailes has arranged the towns of Britain into a hierarchical classification, suggesting an increasing range of functions from the smallest market town to the largest metropolitan city. The emphasis in his work is on the increasing complexity of the market and service function of towns. Other geographers have also been concerned with the specialized functions of most towns and the way in which these suggest possible classifications. It is probably true to say that in all these studies of town regions, of hierarchical functions, and of classification, economic indices have been most frequently used, mainly because of the functional approach, but partly because economic data are more easily available and measurable than social. But there is a growing concern that greater expression should be given to the social structure and dynamics of towns and their regions.

The city itself, its land use, functional zones, and 'townscape', has also been studied by geographers, dealing with it as a complete environment in itself. From the point of view of the theory of the city such studies tend to be sterile unless they contribute to an ecological understanding of the problem. To recognize the city as a product of social forces is not enough without also studying its society. It is social analysis which gives ultimate meaning to the different parts of the city. It is also essential to examine the dynamic aspects of population, the ebb and flow of day and night populations, commuters' journeys, migration. Here the geographer is pursuing an ecological approach, although his ultimate interest will be in place rather than process.

A final concept which is very often associated with the city is that of development through progressive stages, or even of a cycle. Whereas some students carefully dissociate classificatory systems from the idea of an evolutionary sequence, others stress it. Griffith Taylor thought of the city as evolving through progressive stages from youth to old age, distinguishing different characteristics at each and suggesting that all cities passed through these stages. Geddes's concept of the evolution of the European city has been taken further by Mumford, who recognizes distinct phases related to periods of technics and thought in historical sequence. But the idea of evolutionary stages is bound to end in decline. Just as youth passes to maturity, then to senility, and ultimately to death, so Mumford's Western city passes through the medieval, renaissance, and industrial phases and in doing so grows to megapolis and megalopolis and finally to necropolis. Looking at urban growth today it is difficult to escape the notion that growth will continue until the city—in its familiar sense—will be overcome. Already the metropolitan city is a commonplace; already large cities are so voraciously devouring their near neighbours by growth that we have to talk in terms of conurbations; already conurbations are in danger of coalescing, as indeed they almost have done along the eastern seaboard of the U.S.A., giving a megalopolis of frightening proportions. The problems of the megalopolis, or even of the conurbation, are different from those of the city: are they to be more intractable? Is civilization going to destroy itself in this way? Some are certainly thinking in terms of the death of the city. Individual cities have often proved unstable: those of the prehistoric civilizations and even of classical civilization rarely survived. But the decline of the city today is not necessarily the inevitable sequence of a Spenglerian cycle. It may be the logical result of its inability to cope with an explosion of population which is depending on a smaller and smaller proportion of food-producers. It may well be that the modern city's inability to defend itself in war will contribute to its decline. But even now new forms are becoming apparent which show that the 'classical' city is outmoded, and that only rapid adaptation will prevent the present-day maladjustments becoming complete chaos.

2
The Process of Urbanization

(i)

A FIRST TASK is to estimate how many of the world's people live in towns and cities. Living in Britain, our personal experience might give us a biased impression, for in England and Wales, as we have already seen, approximately four persons in five live in towns. Being aware of the problems resulting from urbanization in the developing countries may also lead to mistaken conclusions. In fact about seven out of ten of the world's population still live outside cities and towns. This is a rural world in spite of the fact that urbanization is more advanced than it has ever been. Doubts may arise about ever arriving at very accurate figures because of the difficulties of definition which were discussed in the last chapter. Before we look at the degree of urbanization in various countries, these are the numbers and proportions of the world's people living in towns and cities of a given size (*c.* 1955 figures):

Size of urban settlement	*Number of settlements*	*Pop. in millions*	*Percentage of world pop.*
Over 5,000 people	27,600	717	30
Over 20,000 people	5,500	507	21
Over 100,000 people	875	314	13
Over 500,000 people	133	158	7
Over 1,000,000 people	49	101	4

Urban population is spread very unevenly over the world's surface. Regions of extreme urbanization are few and restricted. The figures by continental regions (*c.* 1955) are given at the top of p. 14.

The high figure for Oceania reflects the great cities of Australia. North America is only a little less urbanized. But perhaps it is sur-

	Percentage living in cities over	
	20,000	100,000
World	21	13
Oceania	47	41
North America	42	29
Europe	35	21
U.S.S.R.	31	18
South America	26	18
Central America	21	12
Asia	13	8
Africa	9	5

prising that Europe is in third place with little more than one third of its people living in towns of over 20,000.[1] Asia and Africa, particularly the latter, where urbanization is recent, are understandably low in the table. Fig. 1 shows the percentage living in towns over 20,000 by countries. The variation in degree of urbanization is infinitely greater when the figures for individual countries are studied according to the local definition of what constitutes a town. They range from 2·4% in Uganda and 2·8% in Nepal to 80·0% in England and Wales (1961), 69·9% in the United States, and 67·2% in Venezuela. To a certain extent the figure for Uganda is indicative of the generally low degree of urbanization in Africa south of the Sahara. Ghana, with 23·1% urban population, is relatively high for this region, and Guinea (8·3%) and Kenya (7·6%) more typical. The Union of South Africa is atypical because of the extent of white colonization, but even so the figure of 45·0% is not very high. North of the Sahara, Africa has shared more the trends of the Mediterranean world, and the percentages are higher than in the tropical belt. In Morocco 29·3% of the population live in towns; 32·6% in Algeria, 35·6% in Tunisia, and 37·7% in the United Arab Republic. Some of the forces which lie behind these differences north and south of the Sahara will be mentioned below.

The extremely low percentage of urban population in Nepal is a pointer to the low degree of urbanization in Asia, though there are exceptions. In Pakistan 13·1% of the population live in towns, 14·8% in Indonesia, and 18·0% in India. Once again the exceptions in Asia lie nearer Europe and have a long history of urbanization: Iraq with 39·2%, for example, and Jordan with 37·7%. For different reasons Japan (63·5%), Bahrein (65·5%), and Israel (77·9%) are quite exceptional. Japan has been experiencing social changes which

[1] 20,000 is a large figure by which to define a town, and the urban percentage would be higher if a lower figure was chosen.

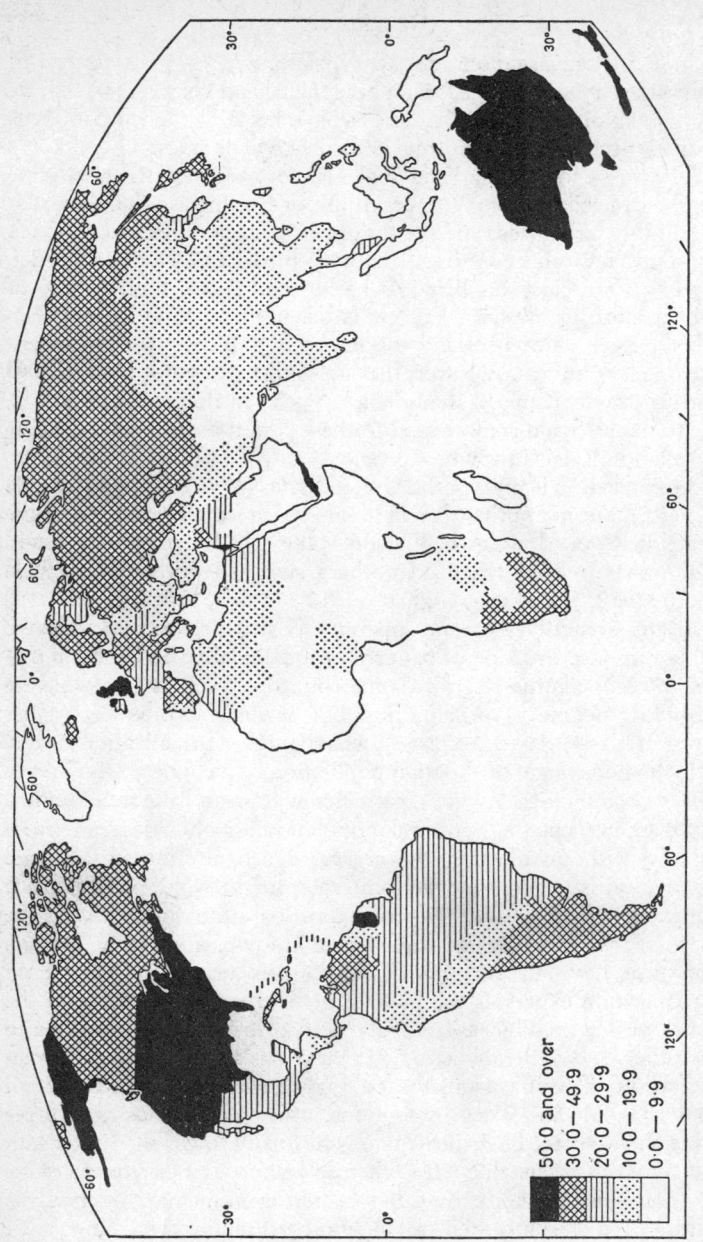

1. *Percentage of population living in towns of over 20,000 inhabitants by countries*

include industrialization and urbanization for a long time, but Bahrein's city growth has been phenomenal and very recent, reflecting oil exploitation; and the Israelis have brought their urban civilization with them from Europe in the last few decades.

The figure for England and Wales (80·0%) represents an extreme degree of urbanization. We may think of Europe as a whole as being highly urbanized but this figure is in fact rather exceptional. Though a few other countries, such as Denmark (74·0%) and Sweden (72·8%), are close on Britain's heels, the general high degree of urbanization in Western Europe is balanced by low degrees elsewhere. Even in Switzerland the figure is only 48·3%; in Eastern Europe it is uniformly lower, though higher of course than in Asia and Africa—e.g. 39·7% in Hungary, 33·6% in Bulgaria, and 31·3% in Rumania. Spain is more akin to these countries with 37·0% of its population living in towns.

Urbanization is high in the United States (69·9%) and in Canada (69·6%), but in South America it varies very considerably: in some states it is very low, as in Ecuador (28·5%), Brazil (36·2%), and Colombia (36·3%), whereas in others, such as Chile and Venezuela (both 67·2%), it is very high.

In this great diversity and apparent geographic confusion, can we find or impose any kind of pattern? Some difficulty may arise in trying to reconcile the fact that some countries, such as India, have a very low degree of urbanization but also have some very large cities. It is essential to be clear on what degree of urbanization means. It is the percentage of the total population of a country which lives in towns and cities. A few great cities will mean little in a country with an immense agricultural population. Such cities can grow rapidly without affecting the *degree* of urbanization if the rural population is growing at the same rate, for then the proportion is constant. Urban growth must be expressed quite differently, as the increase in the *number* of people living in towns and cities. One can therefore have urban growth without increasing urbanization. Urbanization expresses the growth of towns at the expense of the countryside; it is a measure of the shift of population from one to the other. It is generally accepted that this is an actual movement, a migration of people from the countryside to the town, for, with some possible and recent exceptions, town populations do not replace themselves. Their birth rate is normally lower than the death rate, and this means that left to themselves most cities would gradually die. They cannot grow; they cannot even maintain themselves without replenishing their population by draining the countryside.

This has effects which cannot be discussed here, because we are now concerned with mere numbers, but obviously the process of urbanization must be seen as an aspect of economic and social change, and this is where the problems lie which beset countries like those of South America which are undergoing very rapid urbanization. The attraction of the town has varied at different times and in different countries. In Europe, for example, the latest and most rapid phases of urbanization have been tied to the economic aspects of industrialization. It is a varying mixture of economic and social forces which decides the variegated pattern of urbanization in the world today. One generalization can be made for the world as a whole, and that is that urbanization is still increasing rapidly and is likely to continue doing so in the foreseeable future. A century and a half ago only about 2·4% of the world's population lived in towns of over 20,000: in 1850 the proportion was 4·3%, in 1900 it was 9·2%, and in 1950 it was 20·9%. It is estimated that in A.D. 2000 it will be 45% and in 2050, 90%. Urbanization is nowhere near its peak. The rate of urbanization is decreasing a little in the older industrial countries, but hardly enough to disturb the general upward trend. Urbanization is now beginning to affect the peasant agricultural peoples who form the bulk of the world's population. If present-day trends do continue, then we may only be a century away from complete urbanization. This need not mean that literally everyone will live in a town, but that the small percentage not doing so will be fully under urban influences. In this sense England and Wales are approaching more or less complete urbanization. Before even contemplating this stage, and the possibilities of new kinds of towns and new modes of life which it might entail, let us go back to the beginning, as far as this is possible, and trace the history of the process of urbanization.

(ii)

Historically—or, rather, prehistorically—the crux of the problem of the origin of urbanization lies in the question: when does a village become a town? Many have equated this change with the origin of civilization—as we have seen, the words 'city' and 'civilized' have the same root—and for some archaeologists the symbol of civilization is writing. This connotation avoids the vagueness which attaches to the word 'city'. But however it is defined, it is agreed that this great change in the life of mankind first took place in food-producing communities in the Near East. The magnitude of the change was expressed by V. Gordon Childe when he called it 'the urban revolution'. This gives it the same order of magnitude as the preceding neolithic revolution and the much later industrial revolution. The urban revolution could only have been based on the neolithic revolution, i.e., the change from food-gathering and hunting to food-producing. This was the necessary condition of the rise of towns which followed it. Some time between 9000 B.C. and 5000 B.C., in the Middle East, inventions and discoveries which culminated in the domestication of animals and the cultivation of plants enabled men to change their economy: they were able to produce food and live in settled communities—in neolithic villages. Producing food increased the carrying capacity of land dramatically and allowed an unprecedented growth in population. This led, in the first case, not to the growth of villages, but to an increase in the number of villages, each still being to some extent a small self-sufficing community. There is ample evidence of these communities in Egypt, Mesopotamia, and the Indus valley, as well as of similar peasant communities throughout the Middle East linking what were to become the major centres of city growth. Later in time similar changes heralded civilization in Northern China, and later still, in Central America, there grew up (based on the cultivation of maize) peasant communities which would give rise to great cities.

The link between the villages and the city was the ability of the former communities to produce a surplus. Hunting and gathering is almost literally a hand-to-mouth existence and it absorbs most of the energies of the society. On such a simple level every man is his own craftsman, producing the bare minimum of tools and weapons: there is no room for specialization. But the surplus food of neolithic villages not only gave rise to an increasing population, but freed some of the community from the job of producing food. Moreover, the rhythm of the agricultural cycle, tied to seasonal growth, gave rise to periods of intense activity followed by periods of relative inactivity: to a certain extent every man found he had some leisure. (It has been calculated that a present-day Maya maize plot of ten acres produces about 170 bushels of corn a year. A family of five people needs only 6 or 7 lbs. daily, and the total needs, including those of animals, do not exceed 10 lbs. Thus a family needs about 64 bushels a year. Theoretically a standard plot can produce more than twice the family needs. It is this kind of surplus which enabled the people of classical Mayan times to expand and to support so many non-producers. Moreover the work is seasonal. Put in another way, in theory an individual Mayan can support himself on the equivalent of fifty days' work in the year.) In addition to a surplus of food in neolithic villages there must have been a surplus of time and energy. Some villagers could sever their dependence on the soil, relying instead on the surplus of others and giving in exchange a specialized service. Among simple village communities these specialists may well have been itinerant, one serving several communities. But under very favourable conditions—such as those on the Nile—the surplus would have been very considerable; specialization and division of labour would arise in single communities.

In the first instance specialization may have produced only priests and leaders (expressing the organization of groups) and craftsmen. But it is unlikely that these communities could have continued to be self-sufficient for very long. Inventions and discoveries, and consequently the gradual emergence of new technologies, were not to be baulked by the lack of local raw materials. The Nile Valley had neither timber nor copper, Sumeria had little timber, no stone, and no ores. Such materials were available only by trade and exchange. And from the very beginnings of urban civilization in the Middle East there is abundant evidence of such trade. This not only increased the class of craftsmen but created a new one of merchants. The formerly self-sufficing peasant communities were becoming economically interdependent.

It can safely be said that some 5,000 years ago true cities appeared in the Middle East in which were to be found officials and priests, merchants, and manufacturers. They supplied specialist services to larger communities by whose surplus they were supported. They themselves had severed any connexion with the soil, and it is perhaps an expression of the new channels to which energy could be turned that there immediately arose systems of calculating and of writing. These may have been a direct response to the need for accounting, but they were the means of initiating enormous advances in abstract thought.

In a survey[1] of the main features of all the known cities of antiquity, including those of the New World, Childe suggested several criteria, some abstract, but all of them deducible from archaeological data, which distinguish them as truly urban. First, the cities were very much larger, more extensive, and more densely populated than any previous settlements. These are relative terms, and they might not have ranked as large by modern standards. Sumerian cities were possibly between 7,000 and 20,000 in population, those of the Indus civilization probably about 20,000. It is

[1] V. G. Childe, 'The Urban Revolution', *Town Planning Review*, XXI, 1, 1950.

more difficult to estimate Egyptian cities, but they were probably of the same order. Secondly, the city had a different function from a village. Although most of the inhabitants might still be agriculturalists, there were large classes of specialists. Thirdly, surplus was collected from each primary producer to form the basis of an effective capital. Fourthly, this accumulation was symbolized by a monumental structure or public building. Sumerian cities had massive ziggurats with which were associated temples and granaries; the Nile valley was studded with pyramids, the tombs of divine rulers; the cities of the Indus had their 'citadels'; and the Mayan cities their great stepped pyramids and temples. Fifthly, there was a class structure. Priests and leaders absorbed most of the surplus, and in exchange arranged the entire routine of life and death. In the Mayan culture the priests calculated the beginning and end of the year, the time for clearing trees, for planting, and for harvesting. To be able to construct a calendar was true power. The sixth criterion was, thus, the recording of the surplus, the measurement of the year, and writing; and arising from these, the development of arithmetic, astronomy, and geometry. Seventhly, a new direction was given to artistic expression: sophistication replaced the naturalism of the hunter. Lastly, trade was a characteristic of all these urban civilizations, and consequently the manufacturer could become an integral part of this new community, his allegiance being transferred to the city, rather than residing solely in kin relationships.

Childe stressed the fact that the common factors are all abstract, and that there were very considerable differences in the planned structure of these cities. But it was these abstract features, the cultural capital, which were transmitted from the early centres and became the basis of the cities of the Eastern Mediterranean, of Greece and Italy; and, eventually, of the entire tradition of the so-called Western city. The criteria which he suggested for prehistoric cities may well be accepted as criteria for our own cities.

To balance these rather abstract concepts, a concrete description will give us a better idea of what some of these earliest cities were like. A great deal of evidence has been collected from the remains of the Indus civilization, and from it we have a picture of a city of 2000 B.C. Two of the Indus cities were pre-eminent, Harappa and Mohenjodaro, and although they were 400 miles apart the culture was so homogeneous that evidence from both can be used to build up a picture of either. Harappa covered an area of approximately one square mile and was surrounded by a wall. In plan it had a regular grid road system consisting of two east-west streets and three north-south, each about 30 feet wide. This gave twelve blocks. Most of these blocks contained a maze of small streets or alleyways, bounded by high brick walls, and only broken by narrow doorways: for the houses faced inwards onto courtyards. Most of these houses had bathrooms; there was a complex city system of drains, and the houses even had rubbish chutes to the exterior, suggesting municipal control of waste disposal. The central block of the most westerly group of three has been called the 'citadel', for though its exact function is not known, it was certainly monumental, and it probably played an essentially central role in city life. It was a raised brick platform, with its own massive ramparts, and its central feature was a great bath or tank; closely associated with this was a complex of buildings, including a cloister and a great tiered hall, which suggests a centre of administration or religion or both. The tank is still a central feature of many Indian towns, and related to religious beliefs. In Harappa the block immediately north of the citadel is interesting, for not only did it contain the city granaries, but it also had a series of small identical houses, regularly laid out, in contrast to the freer and larger courtyard houses, and strongly reminiscent of the by-law houses[1] of industrial Britain. These have been called 'working-men's quarters', and between them and the granaries are working floors where the grain was ground; there is also evidence of manufacturing. It looks very much as if there was functional zoning in this city, and this was an industrial area with its municipal granaries and mills, possibly cared for by slave labour.

The information that can be amassed from the ruins of Harappa and Mohenjodaro is unmatched in the Nile Valley. Evidence is also slender in Mesopotamia, but here we do have Herodotus's classic description of Babylon. Although by his time Babylon's glory had disappeared, Herodotus conjured up a vivid picture.

The city stands on a broad plain and is an exact square, a hundred and twenty furlongs each way.... It is surrounded in the first place by a deep moat, full of water, behind which rises a wall fifty royal cubits in width and two hundred feet in height.... In the circuit of the wall there are a hundred gates, all of brass, with brazen lintels and sideposts.... The city is divided into two portions by the river [Euphrates] which runs through the middle of it.... The houses are mostly three and four stories high, the streets all run in straight lines, not only those parallel to the river, but also the cross streets which lead down to the waterside.... The centre of each division of the town is occupied by a fortress.... In the one stood

[1] The product of by-laws following the Public Health Act of 1848. These by-laws laid down certain minimum standards of size, services, and planning.

the palace of the kings, surrounded by a wall of great strength and size; in the other was the sacred precinct of Jupiter Belus, a square enclosure, two furlongs each way, with gates of solid brass. [In the middle of this precinct there was a ziggurat of eight platforms.] At the topmost tower [of the ziggurat] there is a spacious temple.[1]

The impression of a compact, dense, and walled settlement is difficult to dissociate from early cities; but Mayan cities were different. Although much later in time—this civilization flourished from about the 4th century A.D. to the 17th—these cities arose in much the same way as those of the Old World, from a neolithic farming community capable of producing a considerable surplus. The grouping of buildings in these great cities—Chichen Itza, Uxmal, Tikal—was much more diffuse. Even public buildings were loosely assembled, and the houses around them had more of a suburban character. Towards the periphery of these cities the residential areas graded imperceptibly into farming plots. There was no strict division into rural and urban. An excavation of a square mile of the city of Landa showed about 60% of it to be inhabitable, but possibly only 15% was inhabited. Even this gives the considerable density of about 1,000 persons per square mile. The area of fairly close settlement might extend over a ten-mile radius, giving a population of 50,000, even if one allows that only a quarter of the habitation mounds were occupied at any one time. There were nineteen Mayan cities of approximately this size. Tikal, Chichen Itza, Copal, and Uxmal may have boasted populations of 200,000. But however uncertain we may be of the extent of the cities, there is no mistaking the monumental climax at the centre. In Tikal the centre alone was a square mile and contained five great stepped pyramids. There were temples, courts, colonnades, and an observatory. The quality of the houses was highest near the centre, suggesting that the priests and temporal leaders lived here, grading down through other rich houses to the small houses of the poorest farmers.

These brief glimpses of prehistoric cities are sufficient to show the complexity of organization and the advance of skills which justify the term 'urban revolution'. They marked a tremendous achievement in the history of man. They did not survive. The cities of the plains crumbled into decay, and were eventually buried in their own debris; only some of these 'tells' have been excavated. The Mayan cities were overgrown by the forest they had once conquered. But

[1] Herodotus, *Histories*, *I*, 178-181. Trans. G. Rawlinson, Everyman's Library, London, 1910.

in the New World, some of the Aztec and Inca cities became the nuclei of Spanish towns. In the Old World, although cities perished, the idea of the city survived, and the cultural capital which had accumulated was passed on to younger civilizations. As Sumeria declined, Syria and Anatolia took over. The island of Crete drew its ideas from Mesopotamia and from Egypt, and gave rise to a civilization exemplified in the city of Knossos. Soon the tools and ideas of civilization were flourishing in Greece.

This is not the place to discuss the cities of classical Greece, but three points concerning them are relevant to the theme of this chapter. (a) We should not allow familiarity with the Greek concept of the city to misguide us into thinking of classical Greece as an urbanized country. Only a minority lived in cities. By far the greater part of the population existed in peasant communities, and there were parts of Greece where urbanization never flourished. Most city states were small; about 10,000 was a normal population, and this figure was put forward by some as the most desirable size. Athens at its height had a free population of about 150,000, of whom half or less lived in the city itself and in the port. To this number must be added 20,000 or so aliens and perhaps 100,000 slaves. But Athens was exceptional. The emphasis in studies of ancient Greece, as of the prehistoric civilizations, has always been on the cities, largely because of the impossibility of calculating rural population. Urbanization, then, was still low, although individual cities were large. (b) The idea of the city was directly drawn from that of the Middle East. All the elements which Childe enumerated were present. They also formed the basis of urban life in Europe as the idea of the city spread throughout the Mediterranean. (c) Physically, too, the Greek city shared many aspects with its cultural forebears. Although the *acropolis*—the defensive site—was important in the founding of many of these cities, as a focus it soon gave way to the *agora*. Sometimes translated as 'market place', the *agora* was more than that because it was the social and political centre of the city, a meeting-point and a focus. When the city of Athens expanded around the foot of the *acropolis*, it grew concentrically around the *agora*, and if there was a road system which could be picked out from the maze of small streets, it was one which was roughly radial from this centre. Here too were the council chambers and temples. The last represented the monumental element in the Greek city, often the only building of any architectural pretension. The temple was of stone—often imported marble—in cities otherwise built of brick. Most of the city fabric was a formless and close pattern of streets dividing huddled groups of houses, irregularly and unevenly built. Some larger houses opened onto internal courts, but the majority formed what Wycherley calls a 'sober background' against which the temples were outstanding. The city was usually ringed loosely by a wall. The essential elements—*agora*, temples, courts— were retained in the 4th century B.C. when new cities were built on a very rigid grid system. Fortunately these new cities were small, and there seems no reason to believe that the adaptation of the city functions to the grid led to congestion.

The Roman achievement in city-building was tremendous, although again the contrast between the immense size of Rome and the comparative modesty of the planned towns which the Romans developed throughout Western Europe is very marked. In Britain a site of 100 acres was usual (Verulamium, covering 200 acres, was large); but Rome covered nearly 5,000 acres. In provincial cities a population of about 5,000 was considered ideal, but this may have been rarely achieved. The striking feature of most Roman towns was their regularity, perhaps an outcome of their conscious planning. The Roman town began with its wall, which usually made a square, and its symmetry was further emphasized by the two axial roads, east-west and north-south. This plan is still retained in modern Chester. At the crossroads was the *forum*, a precinct which was the equivalent of the *agora*, and here too were the main buildings, including temples and baths. Perhaps the peak of achievement in architectural terms was the amphitheatres and circuses which were such an integral part of later Roman city life.

It is significant that urban life in Western Europe did not survive the collapse of Rome. So much had depended on the impetus given by the Romans themselves, and there was often no vital bond between their towns and the immediate countryside on which they had been imposed. The so-called Dark Ages witnessed the near-eclipse of the town. Civilization retracted, and for the time being reposed in the Christian Church. Monasticism alone represented order and continuity in a continent which had relapsed into small, self-sufficient peasant communities. The monastery represented a self-contained life which was often reminiscent of the town, and when urban life reappeared in early medieval times, the church was often the nucleus around which new life surged. In the meantime, those cities and towns which had not immediately collapsed were the mere shells of towns. The vigour and pomp of Verulamium only gradually died away, but within a couple of centuries a village life was being lived in city trappings. When this particular site became a town again its focus was the church dedicated to St. Alban, and the fabric of the church tower was made from Roman bricks quarried from the ruins of the 3rd-century city.

From the 11th century onwards urbanism began its re-emergence in Europe. Some mention has been made previously of the theories which are held to account for this genesis of the Western European city as we know it. Perhaps they have all underestimated one very important factor which was common to the rise of all towns in the previous urban phases, and that is the ability of the population to farm efficiently, to produce more food, to increase in numbers and produce a surplus as well. Behind the urban revival of medieval times lie a series of agricultural innovations which are too often ignored. These include the introduction of rotation in the three-field system; the introduction of oats into the rotation, which in turn switched the burden of ploughing from ox to horse; the introduction of the heavy plough, which opened up new land; the invention of horse-shoes and halters, which made the horse so much more efficient. Agriculture was slowly changing, and in doing so it gave a new basis for the growth of population and for specialization of labour within the population. In 1086 the population of England was 1,200,000. In 1340 it was 2,355,000.

Given such a background of growth, there were two critical elements associated with the birth of the medieval town. One was the increase in the market function. Towns reappeared as more vital centres of exchange, foci for the agricultural surplus, collecting centres for local areas, and points from which services were distributed. The market came to life, symbolizing the close relation between town region and town, and it extended its scope with increasing political stability. As we have already seen, Pirenne argued that the origin of the city—as opposed to towns—was based on the extension of trade and commerce on a European scale, periodic fairs in particular playing a vital role. The part played by such movements and by communications was of great importance, though Mumford would reverse the roles of cause and effect which Pirenne laid down. Mumford argued that it was the revival of the town that was vital in the reopening of continental routes, and that this led to regional and international trade centres. But Mumford stressed even more the second factor in the growth of towns, and that is the need for protection. Necessity led to the wall as a safe-guard, particularly for groups of people wishing to divorce themselves from the protection of a castle. Once the wall was built to protect a community, its attraction for all those not actively engaged in agriculture was very great, even if they lived outside the walls as so many groups of merchants did.

The role of the Church has already been hinted at. It was important in the inception of the medieval town and also in its economic life. At St. Albans the line of Watling Street, which had previously run through the centre of old Verulamium, was deflected north in a great loop so that it would pass the Abbey. Here a market grew. The large part played by the Church as an institution is reflected only too clearly in the towns. The Church must have accounted for much of the population of towns like Cirencester, which in 1314 had 105 acolytes, 140 sub-deacons, 133 deacons, and 85 priests. Associated with the Church were places of learning, hospitals, and alms-houses. The oldest universities also belong to this period— Bologna (1100), Paris (1150), and Cambridge (1229). The church itself was the monumental building which symbolized not only the community but also the surplus of capital and of leisure and labour. It dominated the medieval city, and although it may not have occupied the geometric centre it was certainly central in all other respects.

In addition to the wall and the church, the market place was also of vital importance in the medieval town, and, often associated with it, the houses of guilds of merchants and manufacturers. The ground-plan of the medieval town varied considerably, for generally it was characterized by a freedom of form. Some towns still bore the imprint of their Roman origins. This was so in Chester, where the medieval walls were the same shape as the Roman and where the two axial roads still dominated. Most medieval towns grew from village origins, and their growth was natural and unhindered by a plan. In such an 'organic' growth streets were no more than the spaces which remained when houses had been built: they were irregular and often very narrow. Their narrowness need not imply a great pressure on the land. Although there were cases, such as Edinburgh, where the wall became a strait-jacket to growth and where buildings grew upwards into medieval 'skyscrapers', in many there was room to spare for great informality of layout, for gardens and orchards. Some medieval towns did, however, reflect conscious planning. They were the *bastide* towns, built by conquerors in conquered lands. Such towns were laid out in North Wales after the Edwardian conquest of 1282, and Flint is a good example of the designed chequerboard town. The same pattern can be seen inside the walls of Caernarfon.

Medieval towns were small; again we must not be blinded by the few very large metropolitan centres with which Pirenne was mainly concerned. The largest of Germany's 150 medieval towns had a population of only 35,000. Ten thousand was a considerable figure, and 15th-century London, with 40,000 people, was very large. Urbanization was still comparatively small and sporadic. Urban growth in some cities, it is true, had been dramatic, and these were the great commercial and manufacturing centres of medieval times: Milan, Genoa, Venice, and Florence; Bruges, Paris, and Cologne. These showed a sudden and striking surge. Florence in the 14th century had a population of about 90,000, of which one-third worked in textiles. The city had 200 workshops.

A great increase in the population of comparatively few cities also characterized the next phase of urbanization in Western Europe. These are sometimes called 'renaissance cities', but this tendency to look at cities as distinct types should not suggest too sudden a break after the medieval; for in fact there was considerable continuity, and only gradually was there an awareness that new factors were emerging which were giving rise to new forms. Comparatively few new cities of any size emerged, but here the characteristics of this new phase were emphasized, and Mumford believes these were based on three elements. The first was the growth of capitalism, based on expanding commerce; the second was the emergence in Western Europe of the nation state; the third was the birth of an ideology which reflected the mechanistic and ordered framework of the new physical sciences. The second, in particular, was important because it meant the transference of political power from the individual town to the state, and the concentration in a few towns—or even in one town—of all the bureaucratic machinery of the state. Very often the wealth, culture, and manpower of a state became focused on a single city, a trend which became very marked in the 16th and 17th centuries. Almost suddenly a dozen or so cities in Europe grew to the kind of proportions which only a few medieval towns had reached after two or more centuries of growth. The population of Lisbon, Seville, Amsterdam, Antwerp, and Rome all exceeded 100,000; Paris reached 180,000, Naples 240,000, and London 250,000. Again it should be stressed that this is city growth rather than urbanization; it is doubtful if the proportion of the total population which lived in towns increased. Smaller towns were not very different in size from their medieval forerunners, but now disproportionately minor compared with the capital city of the state. At the end of the 17th century Bristol and Norwich still had only some 30,000 people and York and Exeter were the only other two

English towns which could muster more than 10,000. By the 18th century Berlin, Warsaw, and Copenhagen had exceeded 100,000, and Moscow, Vienna, St. Petersburg, and Palermo had exceeded 200,000. By the end of the 18th century Paris could boast of 670,000 inhabitants and London of 800,000. Regional centres and trading cities remained small, rarely exceeding 50,000 people.

These figures were often swollen by armies and by munition workers, for modes of defence had suddenly changed. The wall, the symbol of medieval defence, had lost its meaning in face of technical changes in warfare. True, the first reaction of town-builders to the cannon was to strengthen and deepen defences by multiplying moats and ramparts and building great bastions (most of which, incidentally, reflected the new scientific precision of the engineer); but these were found to be nothing more than strait-jackets which made expansion impossible. The hallmark of the new city was the long straight avenue which made deployment of troops easy. Indeed the principle highway, wide enough to take an army, was called the 'military street'. These avenues were often super-imposed on a grid system, or made their own radial pattern. The imprint of planning and of logical order was very strong indeed. This response to changed times also gave the city a new spaciousness which was expressed in its monumental buildings. The rise of the sovereign state was certainly reflected in the latter, for pride of place was usually taken by the sovereign's palace, around which was evidence enough of the accumulation of capital—the pleasure gardens, theatres, and museums in which the court displayed its wealth. Where a medieval city already existed this new phase of city growth was often rather like an appendage. The St. James's region in London—the focus of later elegant squares and avenues—and even more so the palace at Greenwich, were quite separate from the city. Versailles was built well outside the limits of Paris.

The capital city contained within itself the seed of greater growth: the court and government demanded their own services and their own bureaucracy, and the effect snowballed until the dominance of the capital city was complete and unchallenged. The glory was a restricted one which was barely reflected in provincial towns except for those which, like the spas, shared royal patronage. Bath was a good example of this and so, rather later, was Brighton.

Massive urbanization was still to come, for the growth of the capital renaissance city had little effect on the mass of the population of Western Europe. The fundamental change was initiated by the industrial revolution. It did not come at once, nor did it have an immediate effect on all Western European states. In Britain it can be assumed that its effects were beginning to be felt at the end of the 18th century, and its peak lay in the second half of the 19th century. It was later in France and Germany and the United States.

The severance from the land, which was the basis of all urban population, had previously affected only a small minority of people even in those countries of Western Europe which boasted great cities. The needs of the rural population for manufactures and services could be met at a simple level; in fact manufacturing was so dispersed and on so small a scale that outside the towns it merged into rural life and in no way disrupted it. The presence of small mills and of workshops was an integral part of the countryside and there was no indication of the schism which the industrial revolution was to bring. But the new needs of industry, particularly for coal and iron, made enormous demands on manpower, and people now began to congregate on the coal-fields of North-Western Europe. In Britain the first half of the 19th century witnessed a great change in the distribution of population, away from the richer agricultural land and on to the coal-fields, many of which underlay moorland valleys previously very thinly peopled. This change in distribution, and the growth of new towns, were the result of an increase in population as well as movement, and this was based both on greater agricultural productivity at home and, later, on the opening up of new lands and new sources of food in the Americas and Australia. Urbanization in the second half of the 19th century would have been impossible without the wheat and meat of the world's thinly peopled grasslands.

In addition to the shift in population to coal-fields, the industrial revolution also witnessed the concentration of people in larger and larger towns. This was partly due to the technical innovations of the period. Compared with former machines—water-mills and windmills—the steam engine was very big and powerful, and its demands in human labour gave rise to factories of unprecedented size. A couple of steam mills could provide the livelihood of a small town: a town moreover which grew almost overnight. Although older towns grew in a spectacular way, it was the new industrial towns which brought novel elements into urban life. They had little to fall back on; they could boast neither of medieval churches nor of the elegance of renaissance planning. For these were substituted civic pride, and industrialists erected monuments to their own abilities and to the glory of the city itself: the great town halls, such as that at Leeds, or the Free Trade Hall in Manchester, were the symbols of the new age. The cities themselves were less glorious, for these people accepted the mill, the gas-works, the soot, and the pollution, as the price of progress, and their industries were scattered throughout the city. The latter was an endless vista of identical streets of identical houses, the product of the standardization of mid-19th-century by-laws whose minimal conditions were faithfully reflected in a million houses which still exist.

This is not the place to discuss the more general aspects of population mobility, but urbanization in Britain in the 19th century was the obverse of rural depopulation; and again the technics of the industrial revolution helped, for the railway introduced a new mobility. Small wonder that railway stations in larger cities were themselves monuments to the new urban age. But the attraction now was not to one city but to many, and the gap between London, for example, and provincial towns began to close. The range of towns became greater as they absorbed more and more of the people of the countryside, and although super-cities emerged, the greater percentage of the population lived in new, and rather smaller, towns. This is shown in the following table (percentages over 50 are italicized):

Percentage of population in England and Wales living in

Towns over	1800	1850	1890
10,000	21·30	39·45	*61·73*
20,000	16·94	35·00	*53·58*
100,000	9·73	22·58	31·82

Soon after the mid-century a majority of the people of England and Wales lived in towns, by 1901, 77% were urban, and by 1951, 81%.

(iii)

Britain was the first country to achieve this high degree of urbanization. In most European countries it is a more recent phenomenon, as the following table shows (percentages over 50 italicized):

Percentage urban population

	1900	1910	1920	1930	1950
France	41·0	44·2	46·4	*51·2*	*52·9*
Germany	*56·1*	*61·7*	*64·6*	*69·8*	*71·0*
Sweden	21·5	24·8	29·5	38·4	*56·3*
Spain	32·2	34·8	38·4	42·6	*60·5*
Bulgaria	9·8	19·1	19·9	21·4	24·6

Germany was the only other country in which the majority of

people lived in towns before 1900. France was approaching it but did not achieve it until 1930. In Europe urbanization is closely coupled with industrialization, and this is certainly borne out by these figures. Scandinavia was predominantly agricultural until the last two decades, and the percentage of the population living in towns in Sweden was still low before the Second World War. Nor should it be forgotten that in Eastern Europe urbanization is still very low. It has increased only very gradually in this century in Bulgaria, where even today three-quarters of the population live in the country.

In the newer countries where industrialization has been relatively recent, urbanization has also been a recent phenomenon, although its increase in this century has been remarkable. This can be seen in the figures for the United States (percentages over 50 italicized):

Percentage urban population in the United States

1790	5·1	1850	15·3	1910	45·7
1800	6·1	1860	19·8	1920	*51·2*
1810	7·3	1870	27·5	1930	*56·2*
1820	7·2	1880	28·2	1940	*56·5*
1830	8·8	1890	35·1	1950(a)	*59·0*
1840	10·8	1900	39·7	1950(b)	*64·0*

Urbanization was a very gradual process mainly because the growth of cities in the eastern states was continually being partly balanced by the opening up of new territory to the west. The frontier did not disappear until the last decade of the 19th century, and so the effect of industrialization—which in any case was much later than in Britain—was minimized. It was 1920 before the majority of people were classed as urban, and this in spite of the fact that immigration had been such a strong element in the increase of population, and that European peasants, towards the end of the last century, were translating themselves directly into town-dwellers in the New World. The rate of urbanization decreased considerably after 1920, but this may be the result of towns spilling over their boundaries as suburban growth increased. The extent of this may be seen in the 1950 figures, for the second figure is calculated on a new definition of 'urban' which includes densely settled urban fringes surrounding cities of 50,000 and over.

In its plan the American industrial city did not have much in common with its European counterpart except for its total disregard for the separation of different functions within the city. The American city was dominated by the grid, but this was not in any way part of a planning process. The division of land prior to building determined the pattern, and the rectangular plot was the easiest and most convenient unit for transferring property, irrespective of the use to which it would be put subsequently.

Outside the industrial countries the growth of administrative and commercial cities also contributed to the increase in urbanization in the world as a whole, and the following table shows that this has been dramatic in the last century and a half:

Number and percentage of world population living in towns of over 5,000 population

1800	27·4 million	3·0%
1850	74·9 million	6·4%
1900	218·7 million	13·6%
1950	716·7 million	29·8%

The large cities were themselves increasing greatly. In 1800 not a single city in Europe had a population of a million, though London, with over 950,000, approached it. By mid-century Paris had exceeded one million and London two million. By 1900 there were eleven cities with over a million people—London, Paris, Berlin, Vienna, Moscow, St. Petersburg, New York, Chicago, Philadelphia, Tokyo, and Calcutta. The two last alone were non-European and they owed much to European influence. During the last half-century the large city seems to have been able to attract population to a much greater degree than small cities and towns, and to be growing, again, disproportionately. This not only reflects the tendency to concentrate more and more capital in large cities at the expense of small and to centralize the organization of national life, but it also shows the capacity of big cities to absorb population and to expand. This is a direct result of technical innovations which enable more and more people to be part of a city and at the same time live farther and farther away from its centre. The last fifty years have witnessed a movement away from the centre, depending first on steam trains, then on electric trains, and lastly on the motor car; but this same retreat has enabled many more to be dependent on the city. The new freedom of movement has led to unprecedented expansion and to a partial disintegration of form.

Returning to the 'million' city—and remembering that the figure indicates nothing more than a very large city—the 11 'million' cities of 1900 had become 20 by 1920, 51 by 1940, 69[*] by 1955, and 80 by

[*] This figure is based on more complete information and more extensive city boundaries than that given in the *U.N. Demographic Year-Book* quoted in Chapter 2.

1961. The last figure becomes 103 if we accept urban agglomerations rather than cities as defined by their political boundaries. This new phenomenon accounts for about 8% of the world's population. In other words one person in thirteen now lives in a million city. One of the most interesting facts about them is that they are increasing most rapidly in the tropical world, although Europe and North America still account for the majority.

Quite as interesting as the growth in numbers is the changing shape of the city in this century. Whereas the suburb was once the appendage to the city, it now often comprises almost the whole city, characterized not so much by new forms as by lack of form. So great has been this trend away from the centre that one is justified in talking of suburbanization. In a closely urbanized country like Britain, one of the immediate results of this has been the encroaching of cities on nearby towns. Urban areas have coalesced into enormous urban sprawls, where the identity of towns disappears, and political boundaries wander aimlessly in solidly built-up regions. In the United States this extensive peripheral growth has for some decades been included in the total urban expanse of so-called metropolitan cities. In Britain Geddes coined the word 'conurbation' to describe the amorphous spread of cities which swallowed smaller towns in their growth. Both metropolitan cities and conurbations are now accepted as urban forms in their own right, and census data are produced for such units. Compared with them the million city sometimes seems small. There are twelve agglomerations of over 4 million, and seven of these are over 6 million. London is over 8 million, Tokyo over 9, and New York over 14.

The logical extension of this trend is the coalescing of metropolitan areas. It has been argued by Gottmann that the entire urban eastern seaboard of the United States must now be looked upon as one great complex—a megalopolis which is staggering in its proportions.

Paradoxically the growth of the super-city is also leading to the possible dissolution of the city as we know it. The techniques which led to expansion, coupled with still more recent modes of communication, may make the concentration of human beings, which has been one of the hallmarks of the city, no longer necessary. It was suggested in the first chapter that the distinction between city and country may be blurred until it is no longer valid. In part the chaotic spread of the super-city is a measure of our inability to come to terms with new techniques. If, in the future, this could be overcome and new forms did emerge, they might be very different from our present cities, and what we call urbanization would no longer be an appropriate term.

(iv)

So far our attention has been more or less confined to the Western European city and its extension into North America. Something must also be said about urbanization in Africa, Asia, and South America, where different forces have been at work with rather different results.

Urbanization in Africa is very undeveloped, and with exceptions it is a new phenomenon. The exceptions are mainly in West Africa, which had what might be termed an urban culture in pre-colonial times. Among many African tribes a town was so called if it was the seat of a chief. They were not necessarily towns in our sense, but rather centres of authority. But, in addition, in West Africa there were great town-like settlements long before the coming of Europeans, and although these often had more of the characteristics of a large village they cannot be denied urban status. However many the farmers who lived in them, they were also centres of exchange, for the town itself, and also for much wider regions. Some were trade centres connected with trans-Saharan caravan routes; others dominated routeways through the tropical forest. All were very extensive and were walled. These are now overlaid by the European-type town which has been introduced throughout tropical Africa since colonial times. With exceptions, industrialization has played very little part in their growth, nor has it been extensive until the last couple of decades. The European's main concern was to set up military and administrative centres and commercial cities. This has emphasized the gap between the levels of the intrusive culture and the indigenous, and there is a greater urban-rural gulf in Africa than in any other continent. As a further consequence African urbanization has several features that are not found elsewhere. For example, there is a constant movement to and from these towns of migratory workers; with exceptions, there is no industrial pull; the usual heterogeneity of urban society is accentuated because indigenous people occupy peripheral quarters which are very different from those of the Europeans, and there is often a multiplicity of races, languages, and religions. Yet however 'foreign' the town is in most areas, it still attracts, mainly because it offers wages, because it is a solution to land hunger, because it offers an opportunity to break with tribal customs. Recruitment of labour is often a means of introducing the African to town life.

THE PROCESS OF URBANIZATION

In the mid-1950s there were nearly thirty large towns south of the Sahara, though eight of these were in the Union of South Africa. They all showed very marked growth in the preceding two decades, Kinshasa (Léopoldville), for example, growing from 36,000 in 1938 to 301,000 in 1959. Ife, in Nigeria, grew from 24,000 in 1931 to 111,000 in 1952, and Dar-es-Salaam from 23,000 in 1931 to 100,000 in 1957. During the same period Johannesburg doubled in population to become a million city. It is difficult to generalize about towns which have such diverse functions and forms as those of tropical Africa, but they are certainly sharing in the world growth of urbanization. It is likely that in so doing they will face economic and social problems commensurate with the cultural gap which has to be bridged.

The percentage of the population living in towns of over 20,000 people is not very much greater in Asia (13%) than in Africa (9%). In general, the countries of Asia are little urbanized. Two countries are exceptional for special reasons: Israel (77·9%) because of its recent establishment and very large number of migrants from European cities, and Bahrein (65·5%) because sudden oil wealth has made it possible to meet the needs of Western technicians. The third exception is Japan, in which 63·5% of the population is now urban, but this increase is very recent. Although we usually couple Japan's demographic history with the introduction of industrialization in the 19th century, in 1921 the percentage of the population living in towns was still only 18·1%. In 1950 it was 37·5%; so the last decade has seen a phenomenal increase in urbanization.

But the great masses of the people of monsoon Asia are still peasant agriculturalists. In India, for example, until recently urbanization was low and fairly static. In 1901 less than 10% of the people were urban, and this decreased to 9·4% in 1911 because of the high urban death rate following plague, and the evacuation of some cities. In 1921 the percentage urban had risen to only 10·2%, and to 12·8% by 1941. Thereafter the figures for India and Pakistan are separate, Pakistan showing very little change (13·1% in 1961), but India showing a more considerable increase to 18·0% in 1961. This is largely a reflection of increasing industrialization, but this factor should not be overestimated. In Asia generally the rate of urbanization, though small, tends to be greater than the rate of increase of economic development. The Asian city does not increase because it exercises any great attraction, though the higher standard of living is always tempting, and so is the need for labour. Rather there is an economic compulsion which makes people leave the countryside, where overpopulation is usually acute; and the city is often the only alternative.

A marked feature of Asian life is the great expansion of a few cities: urban growth rather than urbanization is the central problem. India is still a land of villages which also has several very large cities. There are eight one-million cities in India, two in Pakistan; Calcutta and Bombay both have well over 4 million people. Most of these cities owe their first impetus to the administrative and commercial activities of the English, and few have industries. Commerce is now relatively less concentrated, and industrialization is beginning to have an effect. Of the thirteen cities which showed an increase of more than 300% in population between 1901 and 1951, five were administrative centres and three industrial centres. The more traditional classes of regional commercial centres, ports, religious centres, and military stations, are now sharing to some degree in urban growth. The larger towns have also consistently shown a faster rate of growth. The rate of growth of towns under 10,000 has even declined, that of towns between 10,000 and 50,000 has increased slightly, between 50,000 and 500,000 steadily, and over half a million very markedly. This last group of towns was the only one which did not share in the urban decrease shown in the 1911 census. This means a growing disparity between larger and smaller towns.

The same characteristics, of a low degree of urbanization coupled with the excessive growth of a few cities, apply to China. China has fourteen cities of one million or more inhabitants, and it is in this contrast between peasant life and teeming city that social and economic problems abound. The numbers themselves do not necessarily imply that the city-dwellers need be anything more than peasant in outlook; but the fact that the city population may be largely composed of peasants in itself aggravates the problems which follow urbanization in Asia.

There is considerably more information about urbanization in Latin America than in Asia and Africa, though little is understood about the process and the causes which underlie it. Latin America has a long urban tradition. The Spanish conquerors of the 16th century found a thriving urban tradition among the Maya, the Aztec, and the Inca, and several modern cities are based on their pre-Columbian predecessors. The Spaniards and Portuguese also brought with them some of the urban traditions of renaissance Europe. With so strong an urban heritage cities flourished and their prosperity heightened the contrast between townsfolk and peasantry. The 'new' cities, however, had much in common with the pre-Columbian cities. They were centres of wealth and power, where capital was concentrated, and where the *élite* class lived. The city was usually the home of the landowner and administrator; there was only a small middle class and a large class of artisans and menial workers. One of the outstanding characteristics was the dominance of one city in a state, the extreme case today being Peru, where Lima has ten times the population of the next largest city. In 1942, 29·0% of the population of Argentina was in greater Buenos Aires, and 22·7% of Chile's population was in Valparaiso. Over the whole of Latin America the large city, i.e., over 100,000 in population, is still increasing more rapidly than any other size of town, and there are now seven one-million cities on the continent. Buenos Aires, together with its agglomeration, has over 7 million people. In detail there are variations on this theme. In Venezuela the medium-size city is increasing in number and the ranking of cities is evening out a little.

As in Asia, the presence of large cities does not necessarily mean a high degree of urbanization, and even in the early 1950s only four states had a majority living in towns and cities. Strangely enough Brazil is still not highly urbanized, only 45·1% of its people living in towns in 1960. But the rate of increase in most states has been very marked, and in 1961 in both Chile and Venezuela the proportion living in towns was 67·2%.

Most of this increase in urbanization is the result of migration, sometimes so marked that depopulation of rural areas is considered a problem in some countries. More often the movement to towns is a relief for rural areas, as in Mexico, where land-hunger has been acute. It is more difficult to define the attraction of the city. Only exceptionally, as in Argentina, has it been the demand for workers following industrialization. More usually it is the vague hope of jobs being available in the big city, though this may prove to be ill-founded. In Caracas the new prosperity founded on oil proved an attraction, and once extensive housing and building are begun, this industry in itself attracts more and more migrants. The rapidity of urbanization is usually made manifest in the great shanty-town areas which appear around the cities overnight. The difficulties of absorbing these massive additions are great, though not as great as the adaptation which a rural society must undergo to become urban.

3
Pre-Industrial Cities

(i)

THE PREVIOUS CHAPTERS have been concerned with the city in general, with different approaches to its study, and with a brief account of the way in which men gradually left the land to live in larger compact settlements which we call towns. As soon as we leave these rather academic exercises and examine the towns and cities themselves we are faced with so bewildering a variety of form, function, and development that generalizations seem impossible. But we are committed to looking for common elements; if the shape and function and growth of cities are cultural elements which have evolved gradually and diffused widely, we can search for some distinctive patterns and expect to find certain broad categories. For example, however different a small market town in England may be from a large industrial city, there are certain common elements which we take for granted: we expect retail shopping to be at the centre, concentrated at the focus of roads, and we expect higher-class residential suburbs to be on the outskirts. Moreover this generalization is also true of most North American cities, and of many in Europe. Irrespective of size or of special function, all these towns belong to the tradition of the Western European city, and almost unconsciously we have defined a class of cities. A vast amount of literature is available on Western European cities. They have been classified by function, studied historically, and been the subject of quite intensive sociological and economic investigation; and subsequent chapters in this book will deal very largely with this type of city. Because it is predominantly a product of the last 150 years, and because its growth is so closely coupled with the industrial revolution, this type of city is often called the industrial city. Someone has said that if the neolithic revolution was followed by an urban revolution, then the industrial revolution gave rise to a second urban revolution. This does not mean to say that every town owes its being to the industrial revolution, but urbanization in Western Europe and North America in the last century and a half has certainly sprung from industrialization, and the modern Western city, if it would be examined in the abstract, would therefore be an industrial city.

Nine-tenths of the efforts of those interested in towns have been spent in studying the industrial city. Comparatively little has been written on the towns and cities of Asia, Africa, and Latin America apart from descriptions and studies of individual cities. Only one writer has dared look for the common elements in all these studies—Professor Sjoberg, in a book called *The Pre-Industrial City*. His hypothesis in this book is 'that in their structure or form, pre-industrial cities—whether in medieval Europe, traditional China, India or elsewhere—resemble one another closely and in turn differ markedly from modern industrial-urban centres'. He interprets society as belonging to one of three technological stages: the self-sufficient pre-literate folk-society which has no basis for urban life; the traditional agrarian society based on cereals and domesticated animals, the plough, the wheel, and irrigation; and the industrial-urban. The pre-industrial city belongs to the second group, and is characterized as much by its division of labour and class system as by its form and function. The term also includes a stage in the development of the Western European city, and therefore suggests parallels with European medieval and renaissance cities.

How far are we justified in using this term 'pre-industrial' to signify a class? Although it suggests generalizations which would be true for all non-European cities, it may be better to look upon this as a residual category—i.e., all towns and cities which are not industrial, irrespective of whether they are comparable within themselves. It would be too glib to suggest that all pre-industrial towns are entirely similar. There are similarities, and the use of a single chapter to cover so many cities makes this assumption, but it must be stressed that the contrasts within this group are considerable. While it is obvious that there are marked differences between Oyo in Nigeria or Mandalay and London, we must not underestimate the difference between Oyo and Mandalay. To take one large class and call it pre-industrial may be an over-simplification, but it will serve its purpose if the diversity within it is emphasized.

Some of the characteristics which are present in most pre-industrial towns—though not always together—are the following:

the settlement is relatively large compared with agricultural communities within the same culture, and is permanent; its dwellings are compact, giving a high density; there is a lack of plan and order in the detailed lay-out; a wall or ditch shows the need—or former need—for defence; the uniformity of dwellings, particularly in height, is broken by one or a few large buildings which are either religious centres or palaces. All these are physical characteristics. In function there is an emphasis on exchange and trade, and the market is a centre of the town and of urban life; manufacturing is confined to the craft level and is usually scattered through the town. Unlike most rural communities the society is heterogeneous and is characterized by a class structure based on occupation; class structure is reflected in dwellings, the finer houses being central and the poorest on the periphery. Some examples of pre-industrial cities will show both how these common elements are derived and their inadequacy in explaining all the features of non-European towns.

(ii)

Among the towns which are furthest removed from the European concept of a city are those of southern Nigeria. Although any Nigerian settlement which is the home of a tribal chief is theoretically a town there is no doubt that many qualify in a more restricted sense as large, compact, and permanent settlements, usually walled. Many have over 50,000 people and some exceed 100,000. Morphologically there is an almost complete absence of pattern, for the town is a vast collection of compounds, each of which houses an extended family (Fig. 2a). The compounds vary enormously in size, shape, and orientation, and the streets are merely those spaces which are not occupied by compounds, though in practice some principal 'routeways' lead from the outside to the centre. Here the chief's compound (Afin) may be easily distinguished by its size. Most of these cities have the remains of a wall—or of several walls, for as they grew so new defences were required. Compounds rarely extended right up to the wall because at each stage in growth there were many farmed plots within the walls. The principal market is usually central, near the Afin, but in the larger cities there are subsidiary markets some distance from the centre. These are often the centres of distinct areas within which there are close tribal affinities. They indicate clearly the way in which these towns were often formed, i.e., by several 'village' communities coming together for protection, since when each community has retained a little of its identity. The greatest obstacle to using the word 'town'

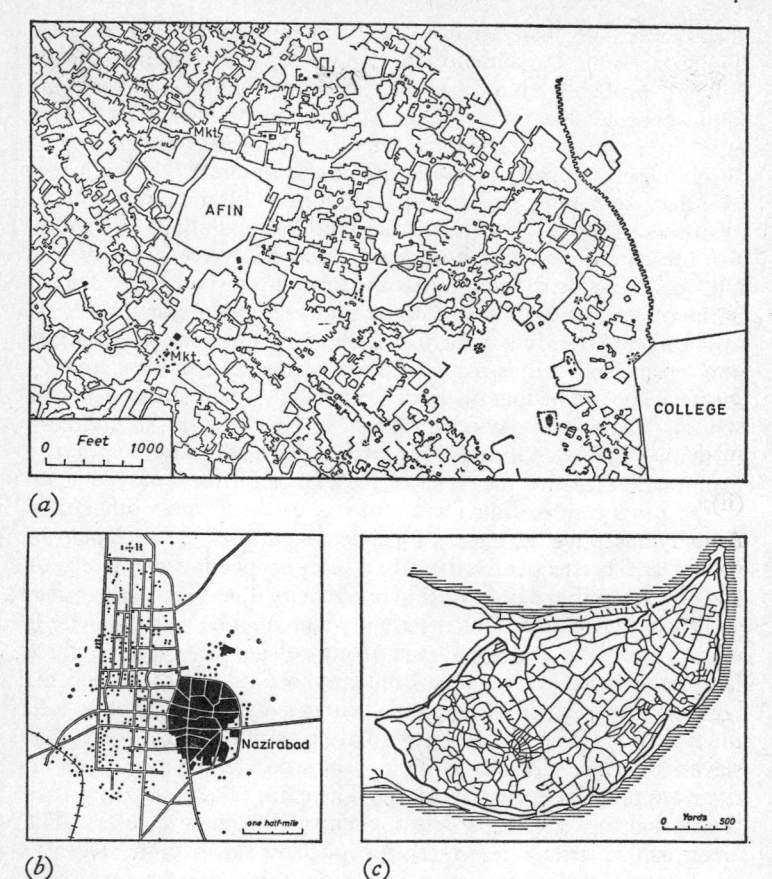

2. Pre-industrial cities: (a) Oyo (Nigeria); (b) Nazirabad (India); (c) Chungking (China)

for these settlements is the fact that the majority of the people who live in them are still farmers. This is a predominantly peasant society which also shares many of the features of urban life. European features—roads and motor cars, more highly centralized markets, shops, and even office blocks—are now beginning to transform these towns, but fundamentally they represent a stage which is less urban socially than physically.

A rather different stage is represented by Timbuktu, where the society seems to share most of the characteristics of urban society. Timbuktu is not large in absolute numbers, but its estimated 6,000 people—probably much less than its former population—is certainly considerable for its situation. It is an important exchange-point in a region where nomadism is predominant. Its people are fairly densely packed in an area of about a square mile, dominated by a maze of narrow streets which are formed by the outer walls of its houses. These are buttressed brick houses, mainly of one storey and presenting a monotonous town profile, broken only by two minarets. Outside the confines of the town are several areas of small beehive huts, some of which are temporary; to the north is a 'suburb' called Abaradyu, which is derived from a word meaning non-urban, and this is made up of temporary dwellings used by Arabs when unloading their caravans. The main market area is central. There is a second market near the fort at the southern extremity, but when the need for protection passed, this temporarily main market became the lesser of the two as business moved again to the town centre. But Timbuktu has urban features other than the obvious physical ones. Its prime function is the exchange of goods, and consequently there is a high proportion of merchants and craftsmen. Furthermore, if heterogeneity is, as Wirth suggested, a prime criterion, then this is certainly a town. The heterogeneity is ethnic, and there are three basic groups of people speaking three languages, in addition to the French who until recently ruled the region. The Songhai, Arab, and Tuareg peoples are further subdivided. For example, the Tuareg have a caste of nobles, serfs, and slaves. Internally the city is divided into quarters, and in addition there are three 'suburban' quarters. The ethnic and caste groups are segregated to a greater or lesser extent within these quarters. The 'suburban' quarters are entirely peopled by slaves or by recently emancipated slaves, and even inside the town those groups who claim an ethnic or social superiority live near the centre, leaving the poorer people to live nearer the outskirts. There are certain secular and impersonal traits in the society which parallel social intercourse in Western urban society. But it was stressed by Miner, who made an intensive study of Timbuktu,[1] that urbanism is not evenly spread in the society. Although the town and society may be called truly urban, there is a range from folk traits to urban traits within the society itself.

There is much in the morphology of the traditional Indian city which is reminiscent of the pre-industrial cities already discussed.

[1] See Bibliography.

PRE-INDUSTRIAL CITIES

For the moment we can ignore the additions to so many Indian towns in the last two centuries of British quarters, which have caused them to be described as a 'collection of period pieces'. Here we are concerned with the indigenous urban pattern, and again the first impression is of great density of building, mainly of brick or stone and usually plastered, leaving extremely narrow and crooked streets which are unable to cope with anything more than pedestrian traffic, beasts of burden, and—latterly—bicycles. The crowding of houses is reflected in the population density, which in parts of central Calcutta and Old Delhi is as high as 450,000 to the square mile, or 650 to the acre (for comparison, Britain's new towns average about 50 to the acre, 150 is considered dense in this country, and over 250 belongs to the industrial slums of only a few of our towns). The vast majority of houses are single- or double-storied, and again the evenness of the town skyline is broken only by the temple and the mosque. The main bazaar is centrally placed, but this is in no way comparable to a Western retail centre or central business district. The retail shops are small, there are dwellings above them and behind, and they tend to spread along the main arteries and develop into subsidiary bazaars. Industry is traditionally confined to small units of half a dozen or so persons, and such workshops are scattered throughout the city with no marked concentration. Socially there is a strict separation of Hindu and Moslem and a marked emphasis on upper-class residences near the centre and on the houses of menials on the periphery. Here, too, the densities drop very suddenly, and the fringes of large cities become purely rural, particularly where they are able to supply fresh fruit and vegetables and milk to the city.

This structure is thrown into sharp relief by the urban appendages which were inherited from the British raj (Fig. 2b). Whether these are military lines, civil lines, or railway towns, the densities are comparatively very light. Civil and military lines are characterized by regular, broad, tree-lined streets, separating neat compounds and bungalows, interspersed with public institutions such as law courts, clubs, churches, and hospitals. Railway towns, in addition to being very regularly planned, have their own hierarchy of house types which reflected the economic and social hierarchy of the railway staffs. Significantly the highest-grade houses are on the fringes, not near the centre. In some of these British sections—which often gave rise to twin cities—there has been centralization, particularly of retail shopping, and this again contrasts with the relative lack of such centralization in the indigenous parts. Density has been maintained in the Indian city in spite of the British example mainly because the vast majority of Indians must walk to their work, except in the very largest cities. There has been no tendency for expansion to be accompanied by lower densities.

The lack of order in an Indian town, with its narrow twisting lanes which on a small scale—as in so many pre-industrial cities—have a romantic charm for the visitor, deteriorates into human squalor very quickly, particularly in the large cities. According to a recent writer on Calcutta, 'At first and second glance, this historic city, and much of the urban sector of West Bengal that surrounds it are among the most unpleasant—even noxious—environments on the face of the earth.' And in this city of 3 million people there are 300,000 homeless, living in its filthy streets, and only 2% of its families have complete houses of their own. It is a reminder that poverty and dirt and disease and hunger are all part of the mosaic of pre-industrial urban living.

China has its spate of towns and cities. A description of one will have to suffice. Until the 1920s Chungking was contained within a wall, though this, built in 1760, had replaced walls of 1644 and 1370; defence had kept pace with expansion. Modern Chungking, outside the wall, has much in common with Western cities, but inside the wall are features which are now becoming increasingly familiar (Fig. 2c): once again the high density of buildings—though this is common in the smallest market town in China, where land is at such a premium that many a town uses a canal as its High Street; secondly, the extremely irregular pattern of streets, though in fact the main thoroughfares are predominantly east-west, following the contours, and many of the connecting streets are nothing more than steep alleyways or even flights of steps. Congestion is severe because pressure on building inside the walls did not lead to building upwards, but rather to eliminating street space. Retail trading is very scattered, but there are two areas where it is not found, for in the west and south the streets are lined by the high walls of upper-class houses, and this reminds us again of two basic social elements, the upper princely-aristocratic class, and the lower artisan-merchant class.

As in India, there is a vivid contrast in Chinese cities where Western influences have been longest felt. The indigenous city of Shanghai is quite eclipsed by the regular near-grid system of the French and British quarters. And when the function of the city became enlarged in response to trade with the outside world, there was nothing in the old city which could accommodate this. The entire wholesale and business sector sprang up peripherally, along the water-edge. And so the 'bund', an introduction of Western merchants, arose as a complex of skirting highways, warehouses, banks, and offices, today marked by skyscraper blocks; this is the true central business district, but quite foreign to the traditional Chinese city.

(iii)

It is clear that there is much in the pre-industrial city of the Old World which compares with the medieval stage of development of the Western city. As far as plan and morphology are concerned there are enough relics preserved in the centres of many European cities today to remind us of the parallel. The medieval wall often survives. Inside was a haphazard arrangement of streets, and the line of the street was more often than not determined by the frontage of the houses. Gardens and open spaces were common, but continued growth often brought pressure on land which resulted in tall buildings, as in Edinburgh, where medieval congestion has left its permanent mark in towering houses of eight and ten stories. Sometimes—as in Nigerian cities, Chungking, and also Paris— walls were rebuilt to accommodate growth. Another conspicuous feature of the medieval town was the market place, and often near by the guild houses of merchants and craftsmen. The third prominent feature was the church, which dominated the town or city. Medieval spires rose high above the roofs of the houses, symbol of the part the Church played in the lives of the people. In many ways the Church represented the worldly success of society, its surplus in energy and capital; but it was also an indication of the dominance of the sacred over the secular. Wall, market, church, these were the three recurring elements in the medieval city which knit together its apparent haphazard fabric. There were, of course, variants on this theme. New towns of the medieval period in Europe, particularly those which were 'planted' in alien territory by conquering rulers, were in some measure planned before they were built, and consequently had a rough symmetry in broad outline. This was typical of the *bastide* towns of the southern part of France, or the towns which grew up in North Wales after the Edwardian conquest. Of the latter, Flint had an orderliness which has persisted to this day; and here, as in Caernarfon and Conway, the castle dominated the town. Another feature of these 'alien' towns worth noting is the fact that the indigenous population was often forced to live outside the walls, forming a suburb which was ethnically distinct. The

Welsh lived outside the walls of Caernarfon. It is difficult not to be reminded of Timbuktu.

The salient features which are similar in all pre-industrial towns arise from common factors: the central market, the focus of routes and the 'raison d'être' for most of these towns; the need for defence which may have prompted density and certainly gave rise to the wall or ditch; the haphazard layout due to a fairly free use of land in the earlier stages when gardens and even croplands were a part of the town. But often interwoven into this haphazard structure, and sometimes even overriding it, there is a symmetry which clearly indicates deep concern with layout, with siting, or with orientation. It would be a pity to emphasize the lack of symmetry in the streets of an Iraqi town, and miss the complete symmetry of its walls. Although inside each great block in the 3rd-millennium B.C. city of Harappa was a maze of haphazard alleyways, the overwhelming impression of the complete city plan is of order and control. The classical cities of the Mediterranean, particularly those which were offshoots of Greek culture, were planned to a degree unprecedented and unsurpassed. The cities of the pre-Columbian civilization of the Andes similarly had great roadways symmetrically dividing them. This imposition of order, often non-rational, is a theme which crops up often in South-East Asia. A little more than a century ago the new city of Mandalay was laid out by court astrologers. Many ancient Asian cities were laid out as models of the cosmos, and in China the orientation of important buildings north to south was extended to many town plans. The crowning example is that of Peking (Fig. 3a). Here there is a city within a city, further enveloped by a city, the centre of the whole dominated by the Forbidden City. The symmetry of the walls and of the main thoroughfares is striking testimony to what has been called 'rational thinking and spiritual clarity'. Although inside the blocks we again encounter the familiar maze of wayward alleyways, the dominance of the total concept is unchallenged. Lesser towns would be unable to realize such idealistic schemes, but we are reminded of the cosmological significance which men give to so much of their work, and that this cannot be ignored in interpreting the pre-industrial city.

(iv)

Earlier in this chapter it was suggested that the term 'pre-industrial city' includes all those outside the Western tradition of the last 200 years. The dangers inherent in such a large category have already become apparent in the immense range of plan, history, and func-

(a)

(b) PETARE Venezuela

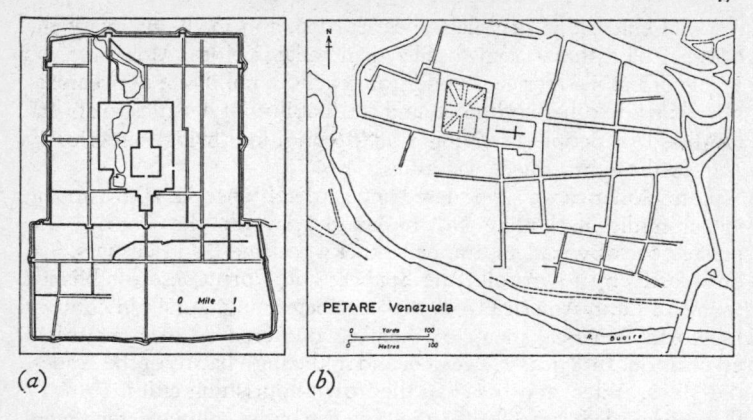

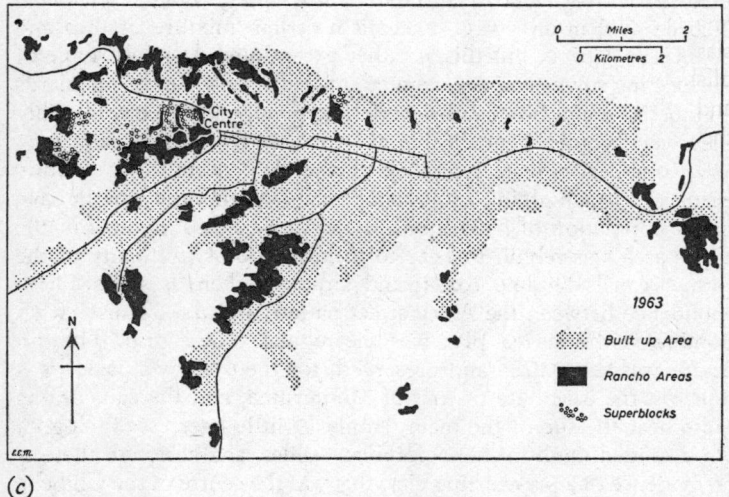

(c)

3. Pre-industrial cities: (a) Peking (China); (b) Petare (Venezuela); (c) Caracas (Venezuela)

tion, though to a lesser degree there were certain common attributes; these have been emphasized. The range increases if we include the towns and cities of Latin America in this class. With few exceptions these have grown from European origins, but until very recently they have not shared those features of European cities which are the result of industrialization. Basically they are colonial extensions of renaissance Europe, and in the majority the original plans have been fossilized in today's cities. Moreover the whole of Latin America is undergoing a more rapid rate of urbanization than any other continent, and the inability of its cities to absorb the flood of people is giving rise to conditions which are closely akin to those in some Asian cities.

Latin America was conquered and settled by people with a strong urban tradition. Unlike North America, where the frontier was pushed back by traders, trappers, backwoodsmen, and farmers, and only lastly by townsfolk, the Spanish and Portuguese established towns in Latin America from the very beginning. Again in contrast to North America, many of them encountered an existing urban civilization. In Yucatan, Mexico, and in the high basins of the Andes, the Maya, Aztec, and Inca had their own flourishing cities. Some of these provided sites for future Spanish cities, though few were incorporated in any way. There is a certain mixture of Inca and Spanish in Cuzco, but this is rather exceptional. Possibly some of the existing towns had degenerated into villages when the Spaniards conquered them. Some cities were destroyed, and more commonly they were rebuilt. Tenochtitlan was founded by the Aztecs in 1325 and, together with its twin city, Tlaltelolco, occupied a swampy island in a lake high in a mountain basin. Together they might have had a population of between a quarter and half a million. But the entire area was rebuilt in 1521 to make Mexico City. Many of the former canals became roads; and although there is some correspondence between the Aztec street pattern and the Spanish, what dominated the master plan was the regular square grid. The old centre was recognized and preserved, for the viceroy's palace was built on the exact site of that of Montezuma, and the cathedral is quite near the site of the main temple. A little later (1538) Bogota was founded, high in the Colombian Andes, and although there is no evidence of a pre-existing city, this was the centre of the Chibcha people and the focus of a fruitful intermontane basin. At almost the same time the first groups of Spaniards were settling the site of the future Buenos Aires (1536). In contrast to Mexico or Bogota this was not the site of an indigenous town. Occupation was desultory and hesitant, and it was a full century before the city could boast of several hundred inhabitants. Incidentally, this sets the pattern for the major Latin American cities. Either they exploited the favourable sites of former Indian cities—and these are almost invariably intermontane basins high in the Andes, as at Bogota, La Paz, Mexico City, Quito, Sucre—or they are coastal footholds like Buenos Aires, Montevideo, Rio de Janeiro. The latter are exactly what one would expect of a maritime European people establishing themselves on a new continent and wishing to maintain contact with their homeland. They were also established in the relatively unpeopled regions, and consequently there is no compromise or admixture with an indigenous culture. These are Spanish and Portuguese towns in the real sense of the word.

What physically distinguishes all these towns is their rigid grid street pattern. This is a system which, as we have seen, comes up time and again in the pre-industrial city, sometimes seeming to contradict the haphazard, organic growth of early towns, sometimes in conjunction with it. It is most often the sign of a town planned before being built; it may make an approximate grid, as in Edward's *bastide* towns in Wales, or it may be meticulously careful as in Greek planned cities. The Latin American grid was taken over directly from Spain and Portugal, and contained much of the renaissance phase of the Western European city in it. It is not the mechanical grid which characterized 19th-century North American cities, and which is merely the most convenient way of subdividing plots prior to their letting. A major contribution of early renaissance towns in Europe was the exploitation of the open space—the *place* or square—and associated with it the monumental buildings of the town. However small the scale, the Latin American city expresses these ideas. Every town has its *plaza*, and in almost all a cathedral or church flanks it, often facing other important civic buildings (Fig. 3b). The plan for Mexico City already referred to had provision for other open spaces in addition to the central *plaza*. Larger cities also had fine main avenues, grander in scale than the subsidiary streets, which again are a renaissance feature.

The centres of most of these cities have by now been transformed by the development of business districts and 'downtown' retail shopping areas. But these centres lack the strong concentration and clear differentiation of American or European cities. Shops and offices are more diffusely spread, and it may well be that further nucleation of retail shopping will be slowed down by the introduction of large supermarkets (*automercador*), which meet parking needs and which are peripheral to the most heavily built-up areas. Around the centre the houses of rich and poor often jostle in the same block. Traditionally the houses look inward to sheltered patios, and consequently the idea of keeping up an outward and uniform appearance matters little. On the other hand the newer suburbs which are developing around these cities have much in common with American or European suburbs: extensive areas of smaller detached bungalows and houses alternate with groups of new apartment blocks, the latter normally having small shops and cafés at street level. But what distinguishes the large Latin American city so clearly is the irregular growth of shanty towns on its fringes. This expresses a particular kind of extremely rapid growth, and has its counterpart in Asia. Some of the social implications will be dealt with later. Here it is necessary to give a little more detail of the physical aspects of shanty towns to complete our generalized picture of the pre-industrial city in Latin America.

Shanty towns—called *barrios* in Venezuela, *favelas* in Brazil, *barriados* in Peru, *callampas* in Chile, and *villas de miseria* in Argentina—are all fundamentally similar. Their growth is so rapid that it has so far defied a reasonable solution. They are always found on the outskirts of cities. They are quite different from slums of the traditional kind, old decayed houses, which may be found near the centre, for they are all of recent origin. The majority are very new: today there are shanty towns which did not exist yesterday; tomorrow there will be many more that do not exist today. They represent the vast movement to the cities of a peasantry, who are attracted to its wealth like iron filings to a magnet. The rapidity with which these people appear is bewildering. The reason for this is that they are squatters, well organized and realizing that only in a concerted movement can they be successful in building their huts on land which is not theirs. Shanty towns arise overnight. Because there is so little available land in any of these cities they appear on the outskirts. One of the most striking features of an aerial view of Rio de Janeiro is the way in which the hill-sides surrounding the city are draped with shanties. In the same way Lima is hemmed in by them, and one cannot approach Caracas without driving through thousands of them. (This is an interesting reversal of the order of things in Western cities, where sites such as these would be appropriated for better suburbs, rateable value tending to increase with distance from the city centre.) Shanty towns are also extensive. In Caracas, a city of a million and a quarter people, one person in four lives in a shanty (*rancho*), for there are 52,000 of them hemming the city (Fig. 3c).

The shanty is a flimsy affair of scrap material—no better, and possibly worse, than the peasant immigrant was used to in his home village. Eventually many shanties will be rebuilt in more permanent form. But for the moment odd scraps of timber, oil drums, zinc sheets, and, more commonly, palm or straw will do.

In Caracas three *ranchos* out of five are made of cane or palm, but usually with a zinc roof. Some will be rebuilt in adobe or brick. Services are pitiful. Roads are non-existent, water is a luxury, water closets rarities. Space is minimal, inside and outside, and the whole *barrio* (neighbourhood) is crowded and noisy. There are no shops; street traders supply some needs, but the city is near enough for shopping. Later, well-organized *rancho* groups will demand police, schools, clinics, water supply—and eventually houses. But these must be fought for. For the moment it is enough that the squatters have established themselves, are now city folk, if proximity to a city means anything, and are on the look-out for the wealth and opportunities which the city is supposed to offer. Too often they must be content with the crumbs that fall from the rich man's table.

The shanty town is both the most distinctive feature of the Latin American city and its most urgent problem. But however desperate the plight of their people, one point must be stressed. These are not slums in the conventional sense, but rather stages in city growth reflecting both the energy and ability of the people. They must, of course, be replaced. During the 1950s Caracas bulldozed thousands of shanties from the hillsides and replaced them with massive blocks of flats. Between 1954 and 1958 over 100,000 people were rehoused. It is a measure of the problem that during that same period 160,000 new migrants came into the city; there were more *ranchos* at the end of the clearing operation than at the beginning. Nor is it likely that the super-blocks are the best answer, for they represent the kind of major reorientation which is the biggest obstacle to country folk becoming city-dwellers. There are many who believe that if squatting could be organized by the city, and if the essential services were laid down before the squatters came, then the use of prefabricated houses would enable the immigrants to do a good 'do-it-yourself' job, and that this would be the real answer.

I have highlighted this particular aspect of the Latin American city, but it is tragically familiar in all the so-called developing countries. The homeless of Calcutta and the refugees of Hong Kong are in an even worse plight. It is the result of an overwhelming upsurge in urbanization in countries which have not the resources to meet these demands, and consequently there is set up a pattern of city life which is repeated in hundreds of pre-industrial cities. In our Western cities housing problems are often the result of age and decay; in the world's young, mainly agricultural nations, they are the outcome of too rapid growth.

4
The Western City

(i)

NOT THE LEAST significant point in which Western cities differ from those of the rest of the world is our own familiarity with them and the amount of information which is available about them. In this chapter the main concern will be with the form of the Western city, again emphasizing—even at the risk of over-generalizing—features which are common to many cities.

There are distinctive patterns of streets and buildings and land-use in our cities which can be explained mainly in terms of the stages of development through which the cities have passed. Only a small fraction of our cities reflect this present age. In Britain, at least, a new town is regarded with suspicion because we are not yet familiar with the kind of town which our way of living now demands. This is natural, for the simple reason that we have inherited most of our towns and cities from the past—sometimes a recent past, but often a very distant past. Perversely, we revel in this in spite of its crippling inconvenience. Our lorries and buses squeeze tortuously through medieval streets; people in the middle and upper classes boast of living in 18th-century houses—if you are very rich you may be able to boast of living in a still older one—and there are millions of people who have to spend their entire lives in Victorian row houses which are old enough to condemn out of hand but not quite old enough to treasure and preserve. There are many towns in Britain which have preserved something from all the historic stages of growth; and if you walk from the centre to the outskirts, you find yourself first in narrow medieval streets, then in dignified renaissance terraces, followed by Victorian by-law streets,[1] and finally in the open suburbs of today. Most towns have well out-

[1] See fn. p. 21.

grown the medieval stage, but some, like Bath, flourished late enough to have a very strong 18th-century taste. The many industrial towns which did not exist before the 1800s will probably be solidly and uncompromisingly 19th-century in appearance. We live and move in the past. The average European city has grown by the accretions of several centuries, and each accretion has maintained

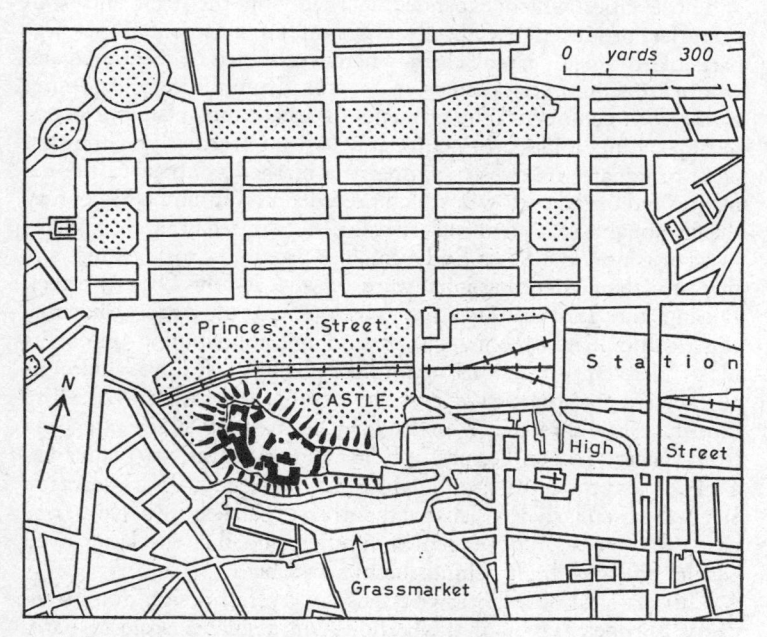

4. Edinburgh: the medieval centre and 18th-century additions

something of its own distinctive character. This is one reason why the study of the development of the Western city is not just an academic exercise.

I have already dealt very briefly with the main stages of city growth in Europe, suggesting the dominant features of each. The medieval core is still to be reckoned with in many cities, particularly where there has been little growth. Castles still exist, walls are intact, market places are still used, and the church may still dominate the city. The walls, streets, and castle of Caernarfon are all intact; the cathedral dominates the existing medieval rows and walls of Chester; and no one can fail to appreciate the fortress-like qualities of Edinburgh Castle or the nature of the centre of that city (Fig. 4). The most obvious medieval feature, and one which often survives even when all traces of wall and buildings have gone, may be the street pattern. Narrow and winding, often seemingly without plan, this is unmistakable. Two historic holocausts have failed to erase entirely the medieval street pattern of London's centre.

Those cities which expanded markedly in the 17th and 18th centuries produced a radically different environment. This was particularly true of capital cities, where wealth was concentrated and whose attraction meant extensive growth. From the very beginning of the 17th century all the elements of renaissance planning began to appear in London. Inigo Jones's Covent Garden was the first *place* or square, its classic symmetry a marked contrast to the romantic and organic growth which preceded it. Within half a century the fashionable section of society was being housed in similar squares in what is now the West End—in close proximity to St. James's at first, but then extending northward of what is now Oxford Street. During the 18th century the development of these residential squares dominated the growth of London, contributing one of its most pleasant attractions. Another planning feature, quite as characteristic of the period, was the avenue. It was left to Nash to introduce this into the West End, in his Regent Street extending from Carlton House Terrace to Regent's Park. This was planned as a whole, and the unity is still evident in the Regent's Park terraces. It may be peculiarly English that this great urban feature began at one park (St. James's) and ended in another, and that the latter even had its 'villages' built behind the great terraces.

This classical orderliness and sense of overall design dominated many European cities of this period—on a smaller scale in Bath, on a larger in Karlsruhe and Versailles. In particular the radial avenues and the convergence on squares or on monumental palaces are unmistakable. Had Wren had his way after the Great Fire, London would have been an orderly grid overlaid by series of radiating avenues. It has been pointed out more than once that in this plan the focus of avenues would have been the Exchange, not St. Paul's Cathedral, but this shift from sacred to secular is more marked elsewhere—for example in Versailles. Wren built his secular monument in Greenwich, and again the size, symmetry, and lay-out of this palace is a clear expression of the age. A century later Jefferson, helping L'Enfant to plan the new federal capital of Washington, sent him maps of all the 'new' cities of Europe, and the result was a striking example of a late renaissance city. In Washington the basic pattern is a grid, but over it is a series of avenues, originally thirteen —one for each state in the Union—tied together by a major east-west axis culminating in the Capitol and a minor north-south axis leading to the White House. Originally there was another minor axis leading to the Supreme Court. Thus the three elements in the government of the country—legislative, executive, and judiciary—were symbolically embodied in the plan. Most of this has been retained, and even today the scale is quite breath-taking; L'Enfant was thinking in the manner of his day when he planned for a city as large as Paris. Half a century later Paris itself was being redesigned by Haussmann, and immense radial avenues began to dominate the city.

Not many cities shared in the classical extravagance of state capitals. For most expansion came in the 19th century, and it is this which forms the bulk of our urban inheritance. So much still survives that it plays an important part in any analysis of the city of today. The industrial city, the direct outcome of the industrial revolution, was the result of a much faster and wider urban growth than anything that preceded it. We are not concerned here with the distribution of these cities, but clearly, as their inception was based on resources such as coal and iron, it followed that population redistribution produced a pattern quite unrelated to that of the 17th century. Some substantial towns which were favourably placed increased rapidly. Manchester, which had a population of about 40,000 in the 1780s, had increased to 70,000 or so by 1801. Thirty years later it had doubled to 142,000. Its greatest growth was in the decade 1820–30. In Belfast, where industrialization was introduced only in the beginning of the 19th century, growth was delayed a little, but was no less phenomenal. A town of about 30,000 in the 1830s became a city of 350,000 by 1900. Other towns grew from almost literally nothing. In 1801 there were only 25 people living on the site of Middlesbrough, and even thirty years later they had increased only to 154. During the following ten years over 5,000 people settled in the new town and from that point it shared in the phenomenal increases of the mid-century.

The growing towns and the new towns were concerned with mining or manufacturing or both. The population of both Rhondda Valleys was less than 1,000 in 1851, living in a number of small scattered communities sheltering on the moorland edge. By 1911 the mining communities here totalled 152,000. Mining was a magnet for hundreds of thousands. But so was manufacturing. And just as the mines themselves were the focus of congestion, so the new industrial techniques demanded an enormous concentration of people. One of the early textile mills of Belfast, built in the 1820s, gave employment to 600 people. With their families they represent the population of a small market town. Such mills were mushrooming in industrial England, and people from an overpopulated countryside, and later from a famine-stricken Ireland, poured into the growing towns.

Our main concern is what this meant in terms of houses and streets, and the first thing which is clear is the extent of expansion in the last century. And as these are the towns in which so many still live—nearly all the houses built after 1857 in Belfast are still occupied—we must take a closer look at their anatomy. Just as the orderliness of the Georgian square and terrace was partly imposed by by-laws governing their building, so the mass of industrial houses in Britain reflects the by-laws of the Victorian era. Previous conditions in the growing industrial and mining towns almost defy description. Gutter Alley in the Belfast of 1837 had nine houses of two rooms, neither higher than 6 ft., the lower floored with earth. In them lived 174 persons. The only reason for remembering Gutter Alley is to remind ourselves what a great step forward the by-laws of the 1840s were. The use of cellars as dwellings was forbidden (in Liverpool, at the beginning of the century, one person in six lived in a cellar), ceilings were to be no less than 8 ft. high on the ground floor, no less than 7 ft. 6 ins. on the first, every room was to have a window, every house piped water. Every house must have a ten-foot-square yard. These and many other standards were a great advance. The 1875 Health Act resulted in further improvements, the chief one of which was the ensuring of a back access for every house. Today we look upon Victorian workers' houses as a blight, and rightly so. But they did mark an unprecedented advance which is rarely acknowledged. Not until the Housing Repairs and Rent Act (1954) was a comparable comprehensive set of standards given to meet 20th-century needs.

One thing a minimum standard is sure to produce is uniformity. The 19th-century by-laws were such an advance that it is not surprising that no one went beyond them. The result is the uniformity and drabness of the English industrial city (Fig. 5a). Unlike the Georgian builder, who composed his terrace into a unit, focused it on a square, or varied the width of the streets, the Victorian speculative builder merely reproduced a standard unit with as few breaks as the by-laws would allow. Mumford has compared this repetition to the machine which so dominated the age. There was

THE WESTERN CITY 57

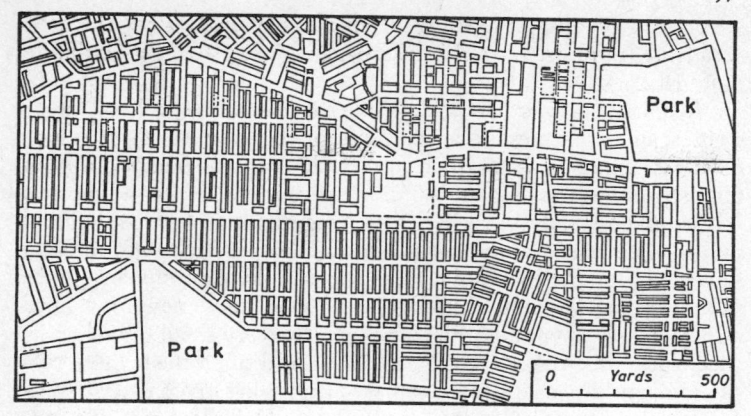

5. *The industrial city:* (a) *19th-century English town;*
(b) *Chicago.*

even an increasing uniformity of building material, for with cheap means of transport by rail bricks began to displace local building materials.

Most large towns had their suburbs, however small, of larger houses, but even these inherited little of the grace of the previous period. Someone has said that you could trust the Victorians with almost anything as long as you didn't give them bricks and mortar. This applies equally to their lack of imagination in terrace-building and to their exuberant romanticism in all other kinds of building. The monotonous residential areas were broken by immense mills and factories, warehouses and gas-holders. If these new towns had a focus it was a symbol of the new age, for every small town had its Mechanics' Institute or its Miners' Hall. And often the symbol of a new civic pride was the town hall. Asa Briggs has given us a wonderful account of the building of Leeds Town Hall. The idea of a new Town Hall was accepted in 1851—the year of the Great Exhibition and perhaps the pinnacle of the iron revolution—and the building was opened by the Queen in 1858. It is a monument to civic pride, and in its way it is as monumental as a medieval cathedral, or as pretentious as any renaissance palace. Its Victoria Hall is 161 ft. long, 72 ft. wide, and 75 ft. high, deliberately vying with other great halls in Britain; for it is bigger than London's Guildhall, and considerably bigger than Birmingham Town Hall. It is about the same size as St. George's Hall, Liverpool, and bigger than the Great Hall of Euston Station (demolished in 1963). It cost £122,000, and had a magnificent organ which cost a further £600.

The comparison with the Great Hall at Euston is significant, for city railway stations were also monuments of the age. In spite of the fact that they are so often hidden behind neo-classic and neo-Gothic absurdities, the iron arches of Paddington, St. Pancras, King's Cross, and other stations are superb monuments, and a reminder of the building which epitomized these new techniques of iron, glass, and prefabrication—the Crystal Palace.

No one saw the drastic changes brought about in the earlier industrial town more clearly than Pugin. Augustus Pugin is remembered today for several early Gothic Revival churches and for the neo-Gothic ornament with which he clothed Barry's Houses of Parliament. But Pugin was also a violent propagandist, a Roman Catholic who lived in an idealized and romantic medieval world and who thought that everything contemporary was base and disruptive. In a book called *Contrasts* he offered a comparison, in drawings, between England in medieval times and in the 1830s. One set of contrasts pictures a town at these two periods. The medieval town is crowned with soaring spires and graced by grammar school and hospital, monastery and alms-houses. The same town in the 1830s has lost nearly all its spires, and its other medieval benefits are in ruins. New monuments tower over the ruins—the mills and gas-holders, the lunatic asylum and jail. Even religious disintegration is symbolized by a multiplicity of churches and chapels of a dozen sects—all built, of course, in the detested neo-classic style. It is a caricature but it contains a lot of truth. What Pugin lacked was the belief which gave meaning to the industrial city and to its sometimes strange monuments, the belief in the new technology and in progress.

In the New World growth was no less dramatic, although industrialization and urbanization came much later than in Great Britain. Here the mechanical basis is apparent, not so much in the repetition of houses as in the repetition of blocks. The gridiron layout is a useful device where the platting of blocks of land precedes building. It simplifies surveying and ownership problems, and is consequently a simple foundation of design. In 19th-century America it also became a method of cellular growth—i.e., a town grew merely by the addition of a number of identical blocks. The commissioners who laid out New York City in 1807 were quite unabashed about their motives: the city was to be primarily for houses, and straight-sided and right-angled houses are the most cheap to build and most convenient to live in. And so, apart from its southernmost tip, where Wall Street is the reminder of how small New York was in the 17th century, the entire nine miles of Manhattan is covered with a mechanical grid. There is no differentiation of function. It was a happy accident that ensured that some of these blocks eventually became Central Park. Chicago's street pattern is even more unrelieved (Fig. 5b). But the system approaches the ridiculous in San Francisco, where the grid is draped over the hillsides and results in the most incongruous steep hills. (There is a parallel in the ancient Greek world, for Priene, in Asia Minor, was laid out in 300 B.C. strictly on the rectangular principle, but on a steeply sloping site that made nonsense of it.) The great American urban monuments came later, at the end of the century, when steel made possible the building of the skyscrapers which now distinguish the central districts of all large cities.

The end of the 19th century saw another trend which contributed greatly to the towns and cities of today. This was the movement away from the town. From the beginning of the industrial revolution, with its ubiquitous soot and grime and squalor, those who could afford to had preferred the sweeter air on the outskirts of the growing towns. They were the few. The majority lived as near as possible to their work. Suburbs were uniformly upper-class. In the last quarter of the century cheaper transport made it possible for more and more people to live farther away. It was the beginning of the separation of work and home which is now such a common feature. The introduction of workmen's tickets on the railways, the opening of the city railways and underground lines, and of the 'elevated' in New York and Chicago, all gave this a tremendous fillip. So did the tram-car. In Belfast (population in 1900—350,000), a million people used the trams in 1881, 10 million in 1890, and 28 million in 1904, when electricity replaced the horse. In the 1920s 100 million used the trams annually, and by 1940 a further 22 million were using buses and 8 million the trolley-buses. Mobility increased enormously. The form of the 20th-century city is partly due to this fact. The result of this greater freedom being shared by the lower classes and the common desire to live in pleasant surroundings rather than in the shadow and under the pall of factories led to the great extensive growth of the industrial city. This was particularly so in Britain, where the reaction against the city coincided with a renewal of a romantic attachment to the land. The English had brought gardens and green squares into their earlier cities; now every house was to have its miniature estate. The middle class, who had been building suburbs earlier in the 19th century, were old hands at creating this illusion, and their larger villas looked more like small country houses. It was they, too, who had set the fashion for semi-detached houses, the first of which appeared in St. John's Wood in the very early part of the century. The idea was that what looked like a single villa in a substantial plot of land should serve two families. In a way, then, the small suburban house, and even the semi-detached, are the final stage in the devolution of the country house, and the smallest lawn is the last remnant of the stately demesne. Improved standards of living, together with mobility, gave rise to the suburbs of the 20th century. No doubt there was a reaction against the overcrowding of the city and against the regimentation of 19th-century row houses. It certainly led to such a weakening of visual ties that the result was chaotic. Mumford has called the modern suburb the 'non-city', and a 'collective attempt at private living'. Others call attention to the fact that with the new mobility most people could 'work anywhere and live nowhere'. And perhaps 'nowhere' is a good description of these

THE WESTERN CITY

suburbs. There is no focus, no plan, no cohesion. Most suburbs have a monotonous sameness and aimlessness that is in no way relieved by the variety of styles of building. Perhaps this variety in house styles among the middle class was also a reaction against uniformity, but the close juxtaposition of neo-Georgian, neo-Tudor, neo-classical merely underlines the architectural collapse of an urban domestic tradition. Perhaps it is equally symptomatic that this phase of growth produced no monumental buildings. One reason is that although peripheral they owe allegiance to the city centre. In themselves they are mere dormitories. The street patterns are negative—half-hearted efforts to escape the mechanical symmetry of the past. There are radiating streets, crescents, squares, but they are uniformly made up of the ubiquitous semi-detached; the plan is an idle doodle in an uninspired builders' office; the radiating streets lead to nothing more than another pair of semi-detached houses.

It is a characteristic of the industrial city at this stage that extensive suburban expansion went side by side with the intensification of land use and of congestion in the centre. Fringed though the city was by dormitories, work was still concentrated at the centre. During the first half of this century most cities, it is true, banished factories and mills from the centre. Mobility has made zoning possible, and new industrial development is to a large extent segregated. In most cases individual factories or great industrial estates have been built on the outskirts, where land values are much lower. Unfortunately this has not relieved the pressure on the centre; for every other function the demand here was increasing as cities grew. Who can afford such sites? A few very rich stores—such as Marshall Field in Chicago or Selfridges in London—or business companies to whom the status value of being in the centre is worth paying for. Are these the monuments of the 20th century?

The office block has long been monumental in America, and European capitals have been following suit since the war. The super office block is exemplified by the American skyscraper. Usually grouped together in a tall core, often very localized, these skyscrapers contrast sharply with the one-storey houses which characterize most modern American residential areas. The development of the skyscraper was partly dependent on the refinement of techniques of frame-building in steel, but also on the invention of the lift or elevator. Both techniques were perfected towards the end of the last century, and the way was open for enormous vertical expansion. New York has as many miles of elevator shafts as of subway, and people travel farther up and down than they do to and fro—and possibly faster. The concentration of people and of land use justified the cost of skyscraper building, but the rise in land values was phenomenal. In the Loop in Chicago in 1880 land was already over half a million dollars an acre. In 1890 it had risen to $3\frac{1}{2}$ million dollars an acre. The functions of the centre, and the apparent high prestige value of its office blocks, have created a vicious circle: more intensive use is justified by higher building, and this in turn increases the value. Even before the end of the last century the intensity of use in many large cities had forced people to move on several levels. A hundred years ago almost all the functions of a city were carried out on one plane: water and drainage and the supply of gas had been relegated to below street level. By 1900, not only were electricity and telegraph wires nearly obliterating the sky, but trains travelled on elevated railways or underground.

The schism between work-place and home, the extension of suburbs, and the intensifying of land use in the centre have together created the greatest single problem of the 20th-century city—the mass movement of people. Paradoxically, improved means of transport do not ensure faster movement. Traffic in New York today is moving rather more slowly than it did in 1900. In London recently a fractional increase in speed to a little over ten miles an hour was hailed with delight; a barrister walked from his office to his home in a North London suburb quicker than a newspaper man who had started from the same office at the same time but travelled by bus. Recently there has been a danger that the central functions of the city might break down completely. The centre is the most valued site because, theoretically, it is the most accessible. The entire pattern of retail trading, for example, has arisen from this accessibility. At all times it was most convenient to have the market in the centre. Lately the competition for the centre has increased with diversification of shopping and with specialization. It is inevitable that the large store will wish to be central. The newspaper shop can be local, because it is repeated a hundred times in the city, but there is only one Woolworths, which must, presumably, be available to all, and consequently must be central. But so, ideally, must municipal offices and banks. This intense competition, which pushes out all but the wealthiest and sturdiest business, arises primarily from the need to be accessible, and centrality and accessibility are theoretically identical. In practice this is no longer so. The centres of large cities are becoming painfully inaccessible.

The traffic problem cannot be dealt with in detail here, but its magnitude and critical importance are only too obvious and are common to all large Western cities. What we are concerned with is the part it plays in the shaping of the modern city. The motor car may be looked upon as a technical innovation demanding new forms. The compromise of one-way streets and parking meters is never more than a stop-gap, because we are still trying to fit this new technique into out-dated cities. But in the meantime the resulting lack of accessibility has produced novel ideas which may be a pointer to the shape the city is taking. One obvious answer is to remove from the centre some of those functions which we have always associated with it, and thus break down what has become a hallowed pattern. The first move in this direction came from the United States, when motels began to supplement hotels. Hotels are traditionally found in the centre of cities, but they can rarely accommodate even a fraction of the cars which travellers use. The answer was the motel, designed to take car as well as travellers, and situated on the approaches to a city—where, incidentally, land values are low. Major American cities are now ringed with motels. They are beginning to make their appearance in this country. In the same way shops are moving outwards to accommodate motor traffic. A shopping parade—which provides most of the ordinary needs of the housewife—outside the city, and provided with a vast parking lot, is comparatively cheap and attractive. This has reached its logical conclusion in those cases where a shopping centre has been built between two towns. This not only emphasizes the shift in accessibility, but it subtracts from the town the very function which was its raison d'être. Drive-in restaurants and cinemas, built beyond the city limits, have all tended to diminish the attraction of the city centre.

Is the city disintegrating? One thing is certain, that the traditional forms can no longer meet the demands of the car, and cities must come to terms with it. Perhaps Los Angeles comes as near as any city to meeting this situation. Los Angeles has always been a very dispersed, low-density city, its several parts only loosely tied together. Now the whole is overlaid with a mass of freeways. The area of roads and parking lots in central Los Angeles—i.e., constantly used by cars—accounts for two-thirds of the total. But in the process the city as we know it has more or less disappeared.

(ii)

We have not solved the problem of congestion, but we have to some extent come to grips with controlling the amoeba-like growth of our cities. The growth of London has been compared with the bursting of a wen, and the spilling-out of extensive suburbs has often seemed beyond control. In the industrial areas of England cities grew until they joined with other cities, and in the process they swallowed the smaller towns that stood in their path. Growth diminished character until one was conscious only of built-up areas. These are the conurbations. Between the wars it was frightening to see the ribbons of houses expanding and then joining up with similar ribbons from other towns, and the green interstices gradually diminishing and disappearing. Somewhere in the bricks and mortar lay the identity of what were once towns. A century ago, Stockport, Ashton-under-Lyme, Oldham, and Middleton were all considerable towns lying about six miles away from Manchester. By the 1920s they were all tenuously joined to Manchester, together with half a dozen smaller towns like Prestwich, Eccles, Farnworth. By 1950 all these were mere nuclei in one vast built-up area with a population of nearly $2\frac{1}{2}$ million. By 1951 the Registrar-General had recognized conurbations for census purposes, and had defined six of them in Britain: London, South-East Lancashire, West Midlands, West Yorkshire, Merseyside, and Tyneside. This kind of development was world-wide, for in 1950 the U.N. population commission suggested that tabulations should be made for 'agglomerations, or clusters of population living in built-up contiguous areas'.

There have been three reactions to rapid and chaotic growth of this kind. The first is the attempt to limit city growth by recognizing green belts; the second, the attempt to decentralize population and industry by creating new towns; and the third has been a new approach to the planning of the expansion and the creation of 'neighbourhoods'. London illustrates all three admirably. The approved green belt is some ten miles wide, its inner margin being that of the existing built-up area. A proposed extension would add five to ten miles to the existing belt, and this would carry restrictions on building to more than thirty miles outside London. Building control within the green belt is rigid, and development carefully restricted. The green belt policy—which has been applied to many large cities—is not universally approved. It is argued that to straitjacket a city is a mistake, and that a series of green wedges would be better and more accessible. However, it has also created a belt of recreation, and should be viewed as a positive adjunct, not merely a restriction.

The attempt to decentralize industry and to resettle population in new towns is more radical. Eight new towns have been built around London, all just beyond the limit of the green belt. In addition, five towns farther from London are to be considerably expanded, and the London County Council had built a dozen very considerable housing estates since the war in or near the green belt. At present the total population of the new towns is about 400,000 but their ultimate population will be well over 500,000. These new towns warrant a closer examination, partly because they represent a fundamental break with the immediate past and also because they are influencing the trend for the future.

The eventual population the planners had in mind for the new towns was about 50,000. They were not intended to be large cities, but 'optimum'-size towns which would provide most of the social amenities of urban life. Those around London had been suggested in Abercrombie's Greater London Plan (1944), and it was thought then that their location outside the green belt would guarantee their individual existence and allow them to grow without too much interference from the metropolis. This presupposed the control of London's population growth and the use of the green belt as a limit; the towns were intended to drain some of London's population and help in the control. The new towns were also to be economically viable, and the establishment of industrial estates was a prerequisite. This would help in the redistribution of industries which were attracted to the south-east. It would also break the pattern of commuting which towns near London already had. The whole idea was meant to change radically the unrestrained growth which had characterized London for so long.

What was new in all this was the scale of the operation and its planned relationship to the city. The genesis of new towns of this kind goes back much farther, to Ebenezer Howard's garden city. His ideas were published at the end of the last century as a reaction against the industrial town. Although there was much in Howard's idea that was romantic—for instance the interweaving of urban and rural which is implicit in the name 'garden city'—there was also economic and social foresight. The town had to be economically viable: diversified industries must be zoned, but, because the town was to be comparatively small, work and home were to be quite accessible to one another (as these ideas preceded the common use of the car, accessibility was based on walking distances). Gardens and parks were an essential part of the scheme, and so was the intermingling of larger and smaller houses. Howard's idea became fact. Letchworth, which he planned in conjunction with Raymond Unwin, was built before the First World War. It is 37 miles north of London and has a population of 28,000. The light and diversified industry in the town employs 13,000 people. The idea was attractive and spread to Europe and the United States (where the first garden city was built in 1916). After the first war another garden city was built. Welwyn Garden City, the core of one of Abercrombie's new towns, now has a population of 39,000, but is not likely to grow much more. Although it has its industrial zone, the fact that it is little more than 20 miles from London makes it attractive for commuters.

Letchworth and Welwyn have strongly influenced the pattern of post-war new towns around London. The reaction against high-density housing in cities is very evident in the low housing densities in all these towns. This is something they share with inter-war suburbs. In Howard's view the light density was dictated by the need for gardens and open spaces, and Letchworth has only 8 houses to the acre, Welwyn Garden City, 11. Twelve has usually been considered a desirable figure even in the suburbs. In the new towns the density varies, but it is never far from 12, the figure laid down by the Walters Committee of 1918. This has led to considerable controversy. Some hold that the most undesirable feature of the 20th-century suburb is the loose-knit character of light-density housing; some have thought that the meagre agricultural land of Britain was being eaten into at an alarming rate as a result. The counter-argument to this was that the average Englishman made such good use of his garden that it actually raised agricultural productivity. More careful analysis has more or less put an end to this debate. The amount of land which is being used is comparatively very small and more than offset by the increase in agricultural productivity. So the discussion of the right density must now be based on discovering and supplying what people would like or accept, or must confine itself to aesthetics and the defence of urbanness. In the meantime the new towns sustained the tradition of very low densities—'prairie planning' was one derisive description—made lower by the insistence of engineers that services be carried under grass verges, so that houses were separated not only by a road, but also by sidewalk, grass verges, and footpaths. Planners and architects are slowly reintroducing urban densities into the new towns. Later additions depart very considerably from the standard 10–12 houses per acre. Fifteen per acre is not considered outrageous, and in one case 20 houses per acre has been accepted. In terms of people, this means an increase from 50 to about 80 per acre. (The higher housing densities of industrial Victorian towns were aggravated by very large families, and population densities of 200 per acre were not uncommon.)

There is considerably more variety in the population densities in a new town than these overall figures suggest. Contrary to the common practice before the last war, when every family was offered the same unvarying accommodation irrespective of its size, houses vary from one-bedroom bungalows for old people to five-bedroom houses for large families. And interspersed with these are blocks of flats and maisonettes. The social mixing which Howard advocated has been tried out in the new towns, but on the whole, however small the enclave of one class in another, it tends to retain its identity.

The third radical concept to be introduced was the neighbourhood. This is fundamentally an American idea, but it made a great impact in this country because it was a basic assumption in Abercrombie's Plan for the County of London (1943). The idea of the neighbourhood is simple but fundamental, namely that one is planning for society and not for an aggregate of houses. It is assumed that when a group of people reaches a certain size it will need a certain minimum of shops, a school, a church, and so on. The unit on which these ideas were centred was the school. Children should be able to walk to school without crossing a major road; the smallest residential unit should support a primary school; large units should contain several smaller ones and be able to support a secondary school. Consequently the neighbourhood is an inward-looking structure, focusing on the needs of the community. Physically this is fairly easily arranged, and it becomes obvious in plan (Fig. 6). Neighbourhoods lie between major roads. Somewhere near the centre are the school and a shopping parade, together with playing-fields, church, public house, post office, and community hall. The latter often houses the clinic and a branch library. About 5,000 was suggested as an ideal population, but some neighbourhoods are as big as 12,000.

This is not the place to explore the sociological aspects of neighbourhoods. It was an assumption that this is the way people live in towns, and too little research has been done to prove or disprove it. Neighbourhood means different things to different people: to the planner it is a tributary area for which he must supply certain services, to the sociologist, an area in which people develop face-to-face relationships. But however doubtful we are about their sociological reality, there is no doubt that as an environment neighbourhoods are infinitely better than the inter-war suburb. There is a logical partial segregation of functions and a provision of

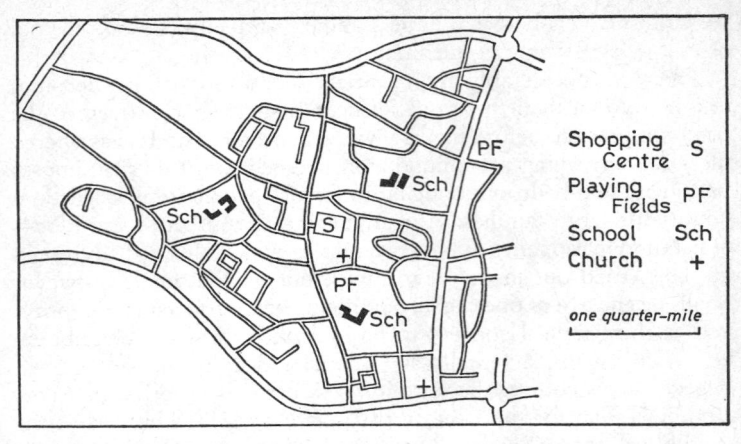

6. *Layout of a neighbourhood in a new town (Hemel Hempstead)*

services which makes daily life easier for the vast majority. It is interesting, however, to see how even the planning concepts have changed. Even within one town it is instructive to move from the earliest to the latest neighbourhood centre: the lavish supply of shops in the first has dwindled to a bare minimum in the last. There has been a return to the idea of the corner store because, it is argued, in a town of 50,000 the centre itself—which has a market where goods are appreciably cheaper—should be easily accessible. In newer towns, then, the shopping function of the neighbourhood is dwindling, and the case is being argued strongly for expressing the unity of the town by stressing the functions of its centre.

No one doubts the great advance in planning for society in London's new towns. Hemel Hempstead is a good example of a fairly self-contained economic unit with diversified industries, and it is attracting an increasing number of offices, so that soon its proportion of white-collar workers will produce a balanced community. The proportion of commuters to London from Hemel Hempstead is very small, smaller than it was before the new town was established. But it is now obvious that the new towns are not the complete answer to London's overspill. Their size—which is arbitrarily determined—is too modest, and they are too near London. What is now envisaged is a series of greatly expanded towns, of about 200,000 people. Six such sites have been suggested, most of them 70 miles or more from London. In addition three cities are envisaged outside the London region with a population from 200,000 to a million. The scale has changed dramatically, but it is much more realistic.

New towns are not only a retreat from the city but an attempt to control its growth. London's new towns were the corollary of the idea that the city's growth should be checked. They channelled population expansion into new patterns and prevented developments of the old suburban type beyond the green belt. In fact it is exceedingly difficult to check movement and communications merely by putting up barriers to the extension of bricks and mortar. We have already seen that in conurbations cities have swallowed their smaller neighbours. What happens when the cities themselves merge? I have already referred to Gottmann's 'megalopolis', which occupies the eastern seaboard of the United States. The area runs from Boston to Washington, through Connecticut, New York City, New Jersey, Philadelphia, and Baltimore. It has previously been described as the Main Street of the United States. Although its nature is diffuse around the nodal cities, densities are such that Gottmann thinks it should be considered as a whole. 'It extends out on a continuously expanding scale, along highways and rural roads, mixing uses of land that look rural or urban, encircling vast areas which remain "green" (and which some wise endeavours attempt to preserve as recreation space for the future), creating a completely new pattern of living and of regional interdependence between communities.' As one unit, it creates problems and makes demands which are different from those of the individual cities which form it. If this is so, then we must think in terms of 'cities' with populations of tens of millions.

(iii)

Megalopolis contains about 30 million people, making even our large cities look small. But numbers may not be the worst barrier to our thinking of the future. Rather it will be the difficulty of meeting new problems while still burdened with the out-of-date cities which make up these new urban giants. Will we stumble along with compromises which will embarrass future generations, or are we capable of devising forms which will meet the challenge? What are the possible ways in which our future large cities may grow? From the many ideas which have been put forward it is possible to distinguish several broad possibilities (Fig. 7). In the first place future city planners could accept the tendencies of the last century or so and even accentuate them by emphasizing the con-

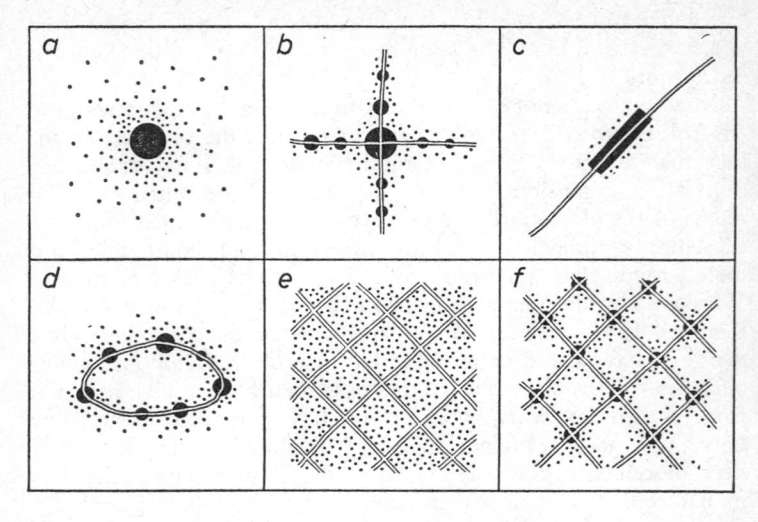

7. *City forms:* (a) *core;* (b) *radial;* (c) *linear;* (d) *ring;*
(e) *dispersed;* (f) *dispersed with nodes*

centration of people and functions. The centres of our cities are already characterized by specialization of functions. This means a very high day-population in the centre, which empties at night, and only recently have cities like Rotterdam and renewal areas like the Barbican in London interpreted the concentration as being in part residential. The core city of the future might have a very high density throughout, both of residences and of offices and shops. The entire surface of the city could, theoretically, be built upon. Under such conditions a city of 20 million people could be accommodated within a circle of ten miles radius. For comparison, the London conurbation, which is bounded by a line of approximately fifteen miles radius from Charing Cross, had a population of just over 8 million in 1961. In other words the density of population would be five or six times as high as it is in London today. The core city of the future may be even more radically different. So far we have assumed a more or less two-dimensional scale, but this need not be so. The third dimension could be emphasized with diagonal and vertical transportation having equal place with horizontal. The city would then be more like an almost solid compact block. New York is a modest pointer in this direction. Frank Lloyd

Wright's ideal city would have gone much further: he himself was planning mile-high skyscrapers just before he died.

All other forms which the city might assume would be the result of extension outwards from existing cores. One possibility is that future growth may be contained along major radial highways. Here use of land would be very intensive and it would allow linear growth along each arm until a star shape would result. But it would also retain open land between the 'arms'. The dominant core would still be the focus of the main lines of movements, and the congestion would be only partly relieved by the subsidiary centres along the linear arms. This is approximately the shape which Copenhagen is assuming. One of the plans for the future growth of Washington also envisaged such a star shape. One plan put forward for the reshaping of London after the war suggested linear growth along main railways and roads running north and south of London rather like ribs. All these plans allow growth without destroying intervening recreation land, and they all maintain high urban densities.

The idea of linear growth is an old one, having been put forward first by Soria y Mata in 1882, but little has been done to realize its possibilities. The essence of the linear plan is a spinal road from which subsidiary roads serve small segments of the city. Form and function change outward from the spine; for example, from shops and offices to high-density housing, to low-density, to schools, to playing-fields. On the other side of the spine segments may be composed of industrial sites. The city grows by adding segments and in maintaining the relation between functions and the central spine. Stalingrad was planned in this fashion. A linear town was planned at Hook for London's overspill, but it was never realized. The disadvantage of a linear town is that the very growth which it is meant to accommodate so neatly will eventually cause both ends of the town to be distant from the centre. On a large scale several centres may have to be distributed along the spine. One possible answer is to curve the linear town back on itself to form a circle, leaving a large open space in the centre. It can then be argued that no part of the town is too far from any other part, either by fast circular transport, such as monorail, or across the intervening open country. The various functions of the town could be strung along the main transport ring rather like beads on a string, and each one could grow outwards if the population increased. One other advantage of such a scheme would be the ease with which the plan of the town could be adapted to topographical variations. In Holland existing towns are being fitted into this kind of framework. Haarlem, Amsterdam, Utrecht, Rotterdam, The Hague, and Leyden form an almost continuous urban area in the form of a vast wheel—or doughnut—the centre of which is empty. The radial system of roads running through this open area would link all the existing centres and maintain a high degree of accessibility; congestion would be shared by all the centres. To some extent the existing towns are already specialized, and if these different functions were emphasized it would tend to lessen the concentration at any one of them. A similar idea has been put forward for the development of Singapore, where new centres strung along the entire coastline would absorb the growth of the island.

High densities are part and parcel of all these concepts, but it is a matter of opinion whether cities should inevitably be dense concentrations of people. Up to the present day this has been taken for granted. The distinction between town and country was formerly a clear indication of two ways of life, of which one depended on the soil and the other was divorced from it; and very often the agricultural demands made on land constrained the expansion of towns and were a factor in promoting high urban density. High density is one of the bases of definition we discussed in the first chapter. The suburban movement, particularly in this century, had militated against high density, and to many it is an indication of the rejection of the traditional city. Thus Mumford refers to the suburb as 'non-city'. Suburban areas degenerate further into an ex-urban area, and the whole has been summed up sociologically as 'subtopia'. To some this situation can only be redressed—both from the architectural or aesthetic point of view and from the social—by the reintroduction of high-density building and face-to-face social contacts. We have already seen that in highly developed countries such as Britain the food-producing argument against extensive light-density building is no longer relevant; and means of communications are such that you need not live on top of your neighbour in order to have close social contacts. Telephone, radio, and television often eliminate distance; perhaps their possibilities in this respect are far from being fully exploited. To most of us the car is the answer to rapid transport. But how can we best use the car? At present it allows us to compromise, by connecting dispersed suburbs and congested centre. Should we rather go to one of two extremes—the compact dense city where human beings are restored to the urban stage but at the expense of the car, or the complete dispersal of the city in a form whose life will depend on rapid transit? Although modern suburbs seem to point the way to this second extreme they are far from being successful, for the simple reason that they have only partially adapted themselves—I almost said accidentally adapted themselves—to rapid transit. Light densities by themselves are not enough. The new form must emerge from a logical system of communications which will also have taken into account every phase of urban life and not merely the residential. We have inherited our present light densities from the garden city concept, from looking at the past. The dispersed city of the future can only arise from planning on the basis of modern techniques of communication. And it follows that what we now think of as central functions must also be dispersed. The basic pattern would be set by a continuous grid of roads which would guarantee a constant flow of traffic: there would be no centre, no terminus. The only city which approaches this today is Los Angeles, though to a large extent the flow-lines are a secondary feature holding together a previously dispersed and amorphous mass of houses which once belonged to several cities. Certainly priority is given there to freeways and rapid transit.

To some the absence of definite centres would be intolerable, and in addition there would be considerable difficulty in locating some of the partial functions such as theatres, centres of government, and luxury shops. Very often the attraction of a city lies in the fact that these are in one spot, and business and pleasure can be combined. The regular grid dispersal could, however, be modified by having nodes of such specialized functions, though these nodes themselves would be dispersed. Some planners think of an 'urban galaxy' of such centres breaking up the monotony of the suburban environment. It is highly likely that this kind of peaking of activities would be socially invaluable, providing the means for the kind of face-to-face and spontaneous contacts which the city has always provided; it is the absence of such nodes in unregulated suburban growth which is so deplored by the advocates of higher densities.

(iv)

So far in this chapter we have been concerned with features of the Western city which have been derived from former ages and which reflect growth and extension. To some extent the city as a whole reflects certain dominant characteristics, but to leave it at this would be to ignore the complexity of the city. What has already been said suggests the zoning of a city by age. Edinburgh is a good example of a city with a medieval core beyond which is a superb 18th-century planned section (Fig. 4). Beyond, and contrasting with it, is the more irregular and dense growth of the 19th century, and beyond this again are the haphazard suburbs of our own century. In many cities only traces of the oldest nucleus are visible, because it will have been rebuilt; its medieval character may be just recognizable on a map, but its buildings will be modern. Street pattern and architecture, dependent on age, will themselves, therefore, give quite distinct areas within the city.

Even more important in giving character to the city are the uses made of buildings today, and it is essential to understand these broad functional zones as a dominating influence in forming the environment of different parts of the city.

The first and obvious generalization is that Western cities have a central core of shops and offices around which are residential areas partly divided by shops along the radial roads leading to the centre. This very clearly-marked centre has been intensively studied in the United States and is generally referred to as the central business district, or C.B.D. Reasons for this concentration have already been referred to, and it is not surprising that as the city grows so does the C.B.D. Spiralling land values have ensured that residential use has dwindled to a minimum. The City of London has barely 5,000 inhabitants. But the core of the large Western city is extremely complex, and it is often easy to distinguish the two main jobs which are carried on there: for most central areas have an office area and a shopping centre distinct from each other. Manhattan has two quite separate poles of activity, the concentration of offices and banks, downtown, and the shops, hotels, and theatres in mid-town. There is a marked contrast in London between the 'City', the business area focused on the Bank of England and the Exchange, and the 'West End', dominated by stores, restaurants, hotels, and theatres. The third element in a capital city such as London is the administrative area—Whitehall.

The office function of the central area has increased enormously in fairly recent times. In 1851 only 0·8% of the occupied persons in London were clerks. A century later the figure was 10·0%. Administration tends to demand a greater increase than business, for with increasing bureaucracy every measure passed by a government demands new hordes of civil servants. This is particularly so in a city such as Washington, which is basically a one-function city. The growth of Washington parallels almost exactly the increasing functions of the federal government: at most times half the occupied persons in Washington have been federal employees—and the other half in service occupations. In most cities the increase in office space has led to expansion upwards, and skyscrapers or tall buildings of some kind are typical of the business area. Paris is exceptional: its upward limit of eight stories has given an even skyline. But American cities pyramid upwards very suddenly in the centre and, on a smaller scale, the Manhattan and Chicago profile is repeated all over the continent. London's skyline is thrusting upwards in a more irregular fashion, the tall blocks forming isolated peaks, deliberately kept apart in order to preserve something of the former skyline. The extent of the concentration of offices, in London, however, is startling. In pre-war London there were 87 million sq. ft. of office space in the central district; today there are 115 million, and in the near future it may well be 140 million. It is a measure of London's financial and business supremacy in Britain that Birmingham, Liverpool, and Manchester all have less than 10 million sq. ft.—although the concentration of the 'business areas' in those cities is no less distinct. Within the former London County, the City and Westminster share the greatest concentrations, each having office property valued at about £11 million, compared with the former boroughs of Holborn and Marylebone (£2½ million), and Finsbury (£1½ million). Although business firms are now encouraged to move out of the central area, the majority are most reluctant to do so. When asked for the reasons why they considered their central location so essential, 78% mentioned the need for contact with other firms, 40% pleaded tradition, and 37% admitted that it was a matter of prestige. It may well be that congestion will overcome many business firms' reluctance to move, but continued growth will certainly be checked by government policy.

Increase in administrative personnel brings with it increase in services, as Washington shows. The West End of London was first a select residential area and later the service centre for the capital. Service functions in general have increased enormously in the last century. In London they now account for about 63% of occupations. Even in industrial towns like Middlesbrough a little over 50% of employed people are now in service industries. Inside the shopping area one can distinguish different specialized areas. Every large city has its Regent Street, Princes Street, or Fifth Avenue; its Broadway or Leicester Square; its Soho; its Park Lane or Park Avenue. These are the areas which come alive when the office blocks have become deserted. The most obvious element is retail shopping. Warehousing and wholesaling are no less distinctive but more restricted. The scores of busy streets in London's West End are more obvious than such places as Covent Garden, Smithfield, and Billingsgate—all of which, incidentally echo location factors which have long disappeared.

One of the interesting details of land use in and near the city centre is the way in which streets or groups of streets retain certain specialist functions, forming small enclaves in the general retail and office pattern of the central area (Fig. 8). Harley Street and Wimpole Street in London are good examples. Here there has been

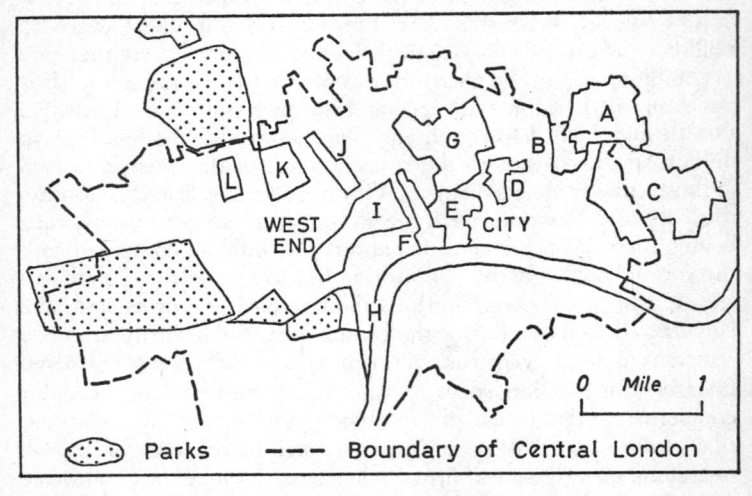

8. *Areas of specialized functions in Central London:*
A. *Furniture quarter*; B. *Shoreditch: printing*; C. *East End: clothing*; D. *Aldersgate: clothing*; E. *Fleet Street: printing*; F. *Law*; G. *Clerkenwell: printing and precision tools*; H. *Government*; I. *Theatres and cinemas*; J. *Bloomsbury: University*; K. *West End: clothing*; L. *Medical*

no apparent change in what was, a hundred years ago, an upper-class residential area. But the number of doctors who now use these houses for consultation have made the street-names synonymous with medicine. On a smaller scale Rodney Street in Liverpool is also an example. More extensive, and reflecting a much longer tradition, are the solicitors' and lawyers' offices around the Inns of Court. These are on the periphery of the old City of London. In almost any small market town in Britain the doctor and solicitor may be found in a quiet back street, near the centre. They have no need for advertising in the market square itself; thus they are accessible without being necessarily central.

The centre of the city is rarely encumbered with industry on any considerable scale. We tend to associate the word industry with immense mills, but of course cities were centres of manufacture from their birth, and it was only the industrial revolution which radically changed both the form and significance of industry. Two hundred years ago manufacturing was carried out in small workshops. The parallel is found in the pre-industrial cities of today. Baghdad has a downtown workshop area in which most of its industry is found. Out of 4,573 industrial plants in the city, 4,449— i.e., over 95%—have less than twenty employees, and 1,661 (about 36%) are shops run by one person only (1954 figures). These workshops are distributed behind the shopping streets, and are often part of them. Some manufacturing sectors in our own cities can be traced to similar concentrations of workshops. One example is the small-arms manufacturing sector of Birmingham. But the best examples are found in London, in the furniture and clothing trades, both suited to the small unit. The former is concentrated in a square mile in Shoreditch and Bethnal Green, where about 3,000 workers are employed in 400 workshops; about a quarter of these employ less than ten people, and over fifty employ less than five. The trade is divided into small, specialized branches, such as turning, veneering, upholstery, springs, mirrors, all complementary but demanding no great factory space. Consequently, former terrace houses have been turned into workshops, and the narrow streets are filled with barrows taking the unfinished articles of furniture from one shop to the next. Formerly this wood-working sector was in the City, but it migrated to its present position when the Regent's Canal began to bring in the timber, and the canal is still easily accessible.

To the south, in Whitechapel and Spitalfields, is a clothing manufacturing district, again almost contained within a square mile. Spitalfields was the former Huguenot centre of silk-cloth manufacturing. The area was expanded by a concentration of Jewish labour. There are several hundred workshops, and the majority employ less than ten persons, again because the specialization on accessories and part-finishing can be done in this way. Some make buttons and buckles, others belts or shoulder-pads, some pleat, some embroider, and some make button-holes. Again the pattern of small houses is undisturbed. In the West End there is a smaller sector for men's clothing behind Regent Street, and a larger and intensive area for manufacturing women's clothing north of Oxford Street.

It is not difficult to see why these industrial sectors can be retained. There is less justification for the heavier manufacturing to be anywhere near the centre, though in many of our industrial cities this is the case. There has been a tendency for newer industry to migrate from the city and most of it is now found on the periphery, though here too it is often engulfed by suburban houses. In London the principal industrial areas are near the docks and on Thames-side, and the Lea Valley is still a centre of industry. But in the 1930s new industrial areas were built to the west of Harlesden, in Park Royal. These are mixed and mainly light industries. There is one distinctive tendency: that when industry moves out in this way there is no shortage of land, so that most plants are low-built and extensive, with a very different profile from the massive mills of the Victorian industrial city.

Little need be said here about the major land use beyond the centre, that is, residential use. This changes character with age and class. Sometimes shopping radiates outwards from the centre along main roads, giving axes to these residential sectors. Nodes of shopping appear here and there, and in working-class areas the corner store and parlour shop are never very far away. Gradually the more congested terraces of the last century give way to the more extensive semi-detached type suburbs of this century. And almost imperceptibly these, in turn, merge into the open countryside. The growth of the suburb has already been discussed. Where does it begin and where does it end? Is it a distinctive area, a specific and peculiar urban form? Some wish to give it a separate existence apart from the town, with its own *mores* and its own mentality. Others see it as nothing more than a point on a continuum from urban centre to rural surround. Physically it is often difficult to see where it ends and where the countryside begins; indeed this merging is one of the characteristics which attract so many. But more significant than the extent of building is the extent of thinking in urban terms, and this goes far beyond any city boundary or built-up area. Few city-dwellers are prepared to live beyond the fringe unless they can be assured of the amenities they have been used to. Fast and frequent train and bus services link apparently rural areas with city centre. The Western urbanite is taking his way of life with him out of the city and into the countryside. Studies of small villages in north Hertfordshire show clearly how they have been transformed and are nothing more than outliers of London. It is characteristic of Western society that urban ideas have penetrated the countryside long before the city itself has eaten into it. It may well be that this very fact will have a decisive effect on the form which the city will eventually take.

5
Size and Classification of Cities

(i)

IN THE FIRST chapter I pointed out that this book would not be concerned with the uniqueness of individual cities but that it would look for generalizations which would enable us to say something about cities as a whole. When faced with a vast number of quite diverse—though related—phenomena, our first instinct is to reduce these to intelligible proportions by imposing some kind of classification. There is no need to go further than ordinary conversation and everyday usage to illustrate this. To avoid going into descriptive detail of a town we will describe it as a market town, or a university town, or a resort, or an industrial town, and may further classify it as big or small. These rough and ready descriptive classes are essential for communication: a bewildering—possibly chaotic—amount of information has been reduced to a semblance of order. To impose such an order through classification is a first step; we must go further, for the classification need not be arbitrary. It may be designed to show the relationship between classes. Let us take a simple example of this. There is no need to study urbanization or geography to know that in Britain there is only one London—i.e., only one city so large that it provides every amenity one would expect in a metropolis and in addition some services not found elsewhere in the kingdom. At the other extreme there are literally hundreds of market towns distributed all over the country. Somewhere in between there are a small number of larger towns which serve regional needs: Bristol, Norwich, Cardiff come somewhere between London and the local market town. The problem facing the student now is whether he can discover a logical arrangement in which the place of each town can be measured. I began by saying that the order is imposed, but it may well be that the order is implicit in the way human societies arrange themselves. We will come back to this in more detail later, but the important points which have already emerged are these: (a) that there may be a logical relation in the number and size of cities—for example within any country x number of small market towns implies y number of large market towns and z number of regional centres; and (b) that there is a spatial relationship between them—i.e., your market town is near your home, and there is an even spread of such towns over the country; but the regional centre may be farther away because there are fewer of these; and you may live hundreds of miles from London. Students of towns and cities have been as intrigued by these relationships, and with efforts to find the simple formulae which will explain them, as astronomers were in the past in finding the relationships between planets which would explain their movements and origin. Before dealing further with our classification of towns, let us look briefly at the attempts made to explain the sizes of cities and towns and the reasons for their particular position in relation to one another.

Perhaps the most obvious fact that needs to be examined is that in most countries there is one city—almost invariably the capital—which is much bigger and presents a greater range of activities than any other city in that country. This phenomenon fascinated the American, Mark Jefferson,[1] who called such cities 'primate', and he produced a law which said that 'a country's leading city is always proportionately large, and exceptionally expressive of national capacity and feeling'. The table on p. 82 shows the size of the capital city of a number of countries together with the comparative size of the second and third largest expressed as a proportion of a hundred. For example, in Spain Madrid had in 1962 a population of 2,260,000. If this were expressed as 100, then the second city, Barcelona (pop. 1,557,000), would be 69, and the third, Valencia (pop. 505,000), would be 24.

In the majority of cases the largest city is more than twice as big as the next largest. In the 1930s, according to Jefferson, eighteen of the world's capitals were more than three times larger than the next city. The table also shows how the disparity seems to be more marked in the so-called developing countries. In Argentina, Peru, and Chile, the gap between the largest city and the next is staggering. To some extent this is true in Eastern Europe, and the dominance of Paris in France is still very marked indeed. There is a historical

[1] 'The Law of the Primate City', *Geographical Review*, XXIX, 1939.

Country	Pop. of biggest city in 000's	Ratio of 2nd city	Ratio of 3rd city
1. Egypt	3,348	8	6
2. Hungary	1,830	8	7
3. Peru	1,715	9	9
4. Argentina	1,700	10	6
5. Denmark	1,264	10	9
6. Rumania	1,355	12	12
7. France	6,524	13	12
8. Chile	1,900	14	8
9. Austria	1,627	15	12
10. Iran	1,838	17	14
11. Mexico	4,666	17	14
12. Philippines	1,138	22	20
13. Belgium	1,019	25	17
14. Bulgaria	695	26	21
15. Finland	458	28	28
16. United Kingdom	8,171	29	28
17. Japan	9,936	31	16
18. Czechoslovakia	1,005	31	24
19. Venezuela	1,336	32	15
20. Indonesia	2,906	34	33
21. U.S.A.	14,115	46	42
22. Algeria	833	47	27
23. Korea	2,444	48	27
24. Sweden	807	50	30
25. Colombia	1,329	52	52
26. Ghana	337	53	22
27. Germany	3,261	56	33
28. Poland	1,162	62	42
29. Spain	2,260	69	24
30. Italy	1,581	73	55

(From *U.N. Demographic Year-Book 1962*)

---

explanation for some of the more disparate figures. The disproportionate size of Vienna is a reflection of the fact that it was for so long the imperial capital of an empire in central Europe. The comparative lack of dominance of Madrid and Rome can also be explained. Madrid, established by Philip II, was in a sense an artificial capital which symbolized the unification of Spain; but it was—and is—remote from the rich agricultural areas of Spain, which maintain cities with populations which Madrid has only recently passed.

Similarly Rome became a capital only in 1870, as an expression of a new unity which switched the focus of the nation from the heavily populated north. Florence was the previous capital, and Turin the first capital of the Kingdom of Italy. During the first three decades or so of this century Rome was only marginally greater in population than Milan and Naples. But since then Rome has increased rapidly. Since the 1930s Naples has grown from 866,000 to 1,180,000 (32%), Milan from 1,116,000 to 1,581,000 (42%), and Rome from 1,156,000 to 2,161,000 (87%).

Although Jefferson assumed that the capital is the largest city, this need not be so in federal countries. Washington (1,808,000) is much smaller than New York (14,115,000), Ottawa (199,000) than Montreal (1,003,000), and Canberra (21,000) than Sydney (1,550,000). In each case, however, state capitals would fit the law.

Jefferson was concerned almost exclusively with the pre-eminence of the primate city. Others have extended the range to examine the size relationship between all cities in a given country. Perhaps the best known study is that of G. K. Zipf. It is noteworthy that Zipf and others were not particularly interested in the city as such, but in human behaviour patterns, and merely used city size as one example in more general theses. In his rank-size rule, Zipf merely says that if you arrange all the cities of any country in descending order by population, then there is a regular ratio between the position of each and its size proportionate to the largest city. The second city in the series is half the size of the first, the fourth is one-quarter, the eighth one-eighth, and so on. It is surprising how nearly this rule fits the cities of the United States. For example, the four hundred and first town in the series (1940 census) is Sharon. According to the rank-size rule its population should be $\frac{1}{401}$ of that of New York City: this gives a figure of 21,600, whereas Sharon's actual population was 25,600.

It is obvious that the law of the primate city and the rank-size rule describe rather different phenomena, one emphasizing the dominance of one city at the expense of all others, and the second giving a much greater emphasis to cities subsidiary to the capital. Jefferson's law is more applicable to agricultural developing countries, whereas our example of the rank-size rule was from the United States, an advanced industrial country. The table at the top of p. 84 compares the number of towns in different categories in two strongly contrasting countries: Turkey, and England and Wales.

The dominating position of Ankara in Turkey is further emphasized by the small number of medium-sized towns (c) and (d),

Class by population	Turkey (1955) No. of towns	Pop. in 000's	England and Wales (1961) No. of towns	Pop. in 000's
a 500,000+	1	1,269	5	6,219
b 100–500,000	5	1,165	62	10,418
c 50–100,000	11	763	117	7,921
d 20–50,000	38	1,181	231	7,375
e 10–20,000	72	1,046	215	3,156
f 5–10,000	148	994	163	1,188
g 2–5,000	616	1,757	139	490

and the very large number of small towns. In England and Wales, on the other hand, Birmingham, Manchester, and Liverpool are all over a million, and the largest single class is 20,000–50,000. This simple equation of the primate city relationship in the developing countries and the rank-size rule relationship in industrial countries is, however, not constant. Countries like India, China, and Korea approach more nearly to the rank-size rule distribution whereas, as we have already seen, Austria—and also Denmark, Sweden, and the Netherlands—have a primate distribution. There is evidence to show that there is no *necessary* relation between city-size distribution and economic development, or between it and degree of urbanization. Yet it does seem as if, historically, countries progress from primate distribution to rank-size rule. In Tudor England London certainly predominated to the same degree as Ankara does in present-day Turkey. There seem to be stages through which a country progresses, and the orderly rank-size relationship seems to be the last. This may be the result of the increasing complexity of urban structure. A small country with a simple agricultural economy can be run by one city which provides the entire range of urban activities, political, industrial, economic, and social. More advanced economies are much more complex and more diversified. Manufacturing alone will set up new foci and attract population, and other functions may split up, producing cities with specialist activities like education or trade, and even government, as at Brasilia and Washington. The job of running the country becomes much more dispersed, and consequently other cities arise which attain considerable size. Such a change, however slight, has become apparent recently in some developing countries. The following table of the numbers of cities in various size-classes in Venezuela illustrates this:

Distribution of towns in Venezuela by population classes, 1936–1961

Class by population	1936 No.	%	1950 No.	%	1961 No.	%
a 200,000+	1	1·2	2	1·2	2	0·8
b 100–200,000	1	1·2	1	0·6	5	2·3
c 50–100,000	—	—	4	2·3	12	5·2
d 20–50,000	7	8·7	16	9·4	25	10·8
e 10–20,000	6	7·4	18	10·6	33	14·2
f 5–10,000	20	24·7	41	24·1	51	22·1
g 2,500–5,000	46	56·8	88	51·8	103	44·6
	81	100·0	170	100·0	231	100·0

(ii)

But our cities are not arranged neatly in tables: they are placed in space. Is there a similar logic underlying their distribution and suggesting a pattern which has arisen from their size-relationships? The simplest situation one can possibly imagine is that of a single city set in a uniform agricultural hinterland. Early in the last century Van Thünen produced such a highly hypothetical model and suggested that man's economic activities were concentrically arranged because they depended upon distance from the centre. Given a uniform circle of land, then at its centre would be a city. Apart from stressing the relationship between city and tributary area, this idea was no more than a starting-point for subsequent studies. It was Walter Christaller who, some thirty years ago, worked out a hypothetical scheme which has been the basis of most modern ideas on the subject, and his so-called 'central place theory' has been quite fruitful. Beginning with the simple assumptions (a) that a certain amount of land will support a town, and (b) that the bigger the area the bigger the town, Christaller went further and suggested that several small tributary areas focusing on small towns would be found within a large tributary area focusing on one central city. Moreover, even in an abstract and idealized pattern of tributary areas, the circle proved an awkward shape and was replaced by the hexagon. Tributary areas now assumed complex geometrical patterns of smaller interlocking hexagons within larger (Fig. 9).

In establishing the framework the first step was to classify the service centres, towns, and cities by size, then compute theoretically their distance apart, and the size and population of the hinterlands. These are shown in the following table:

Settlement	Av. pop.	Kms. Distance apart	Size of tributary area (sq. kms.)	Population of tributary area
Market hamlet	800	7	45	2,700
Township centre	1,500	12	135	8,100
County seat	3,500	21	400	24,000
District city	9,000	36	1,200	75,000
Small state capital	27,000	62	2,600	225,000
Provincial head city	90,000	108	10,800	625,000
Regional capital city	300,000	186	32,400	2,025,000

Christaller's data were calculated for southern Germany, and the regular hexagonal pattern which resulted fitted the facts fairly well. He claimed that the pattern would extend to the whole of Western Europe, but at best it must be looked upon as a theoretical distribution which possibly applies fairly well in a poor agricultural area which has not been greatly disturbed by technological change.

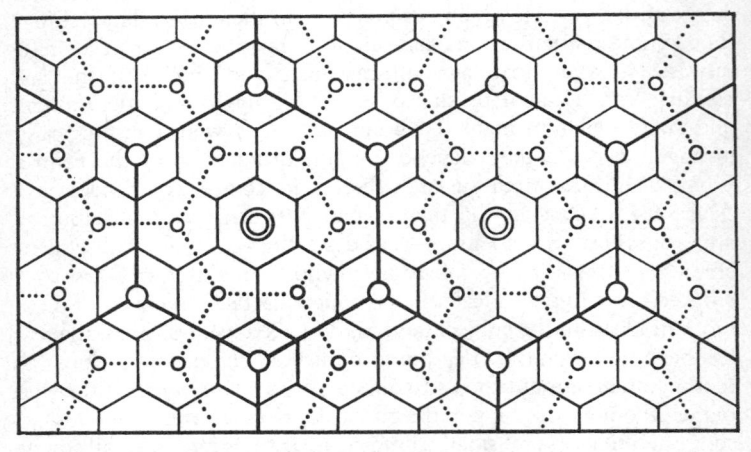

9. Christaller's hexagonal hierarchy of regions

Christaller himself recognized the modifications caused by roads and rail, and that the idealized grid gave little scope for changes by industrialization, or for towns with specialized functions—like education—which have no great local significance. Recently the urban network of France has been analysed in this way, and it shows some resemblance to a theoretical pattern of the kind Christaller suggests (Fig. 10). Cities of over 100,000 people were chosen

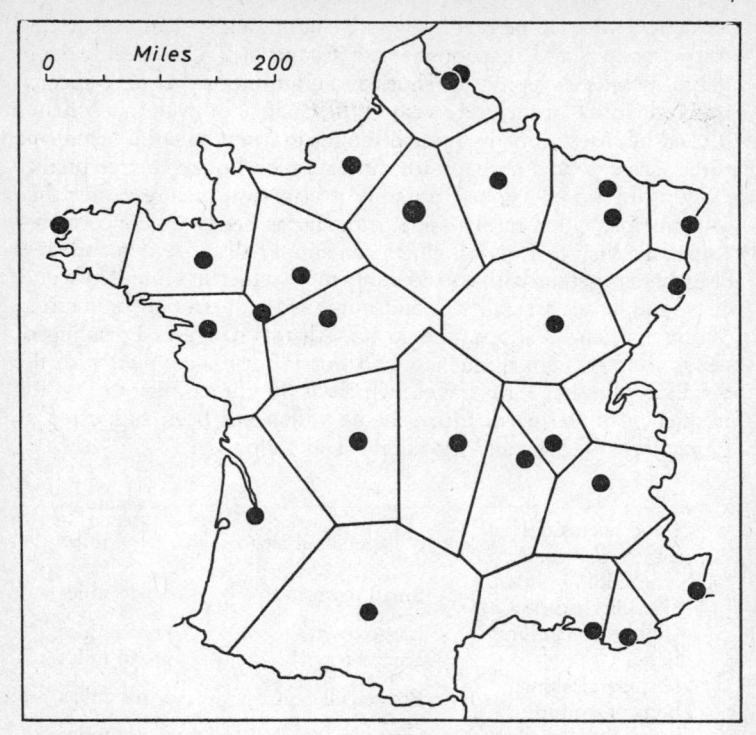

10. *The city regions of France*

as centres; distances between them were bisected and lines drawn through these points. The result is a series of polygons which are very approximately equal in size covering the country in a very broad mesh.

Implicit in the rank-size rule and in Christaller's hexagonal pattern is the assumption that regularities do exist, and, specialization apart, that these arise from the varying demands of society. One of the main functions of a town—or any service centre—is to supply the needs of the population around it. Our needs, as individuals and families, vary enormously. Some services are in constant day-to-day demand—such as basic foods, newspapers, confectionery, chemist supplies, a public house, a post office: these must be within the shortest possible distance and consequently must have a very frequent and wide distribution. For less immediate needs which could be met by weekly marketing we are prepared to travel farther, and, obviously, less frequently. The weekly jaunt might include shopping for shoes and clothing or the more specialized foodstuffs, or include a visit to the cinema, or even to a solicitor if need be. Occasionally a much longer journey must be taken to a really large town, perhaps for furniture or books, better-quality clothing or jewellery, and possibly a visit to a theatre rather than to a cinema. Quite rarely—at least as far as needs are concerned—comes the visit to London which can supply all those demands met elsewhere together with considerably more which are found nowhere else—the larger art galleries and museums, government ministries, highly specialized shops, and so on. All this suggests a grading of needs coupled with frequency, and this in turn is coupled with the distance you have to travel, which is in direct relation to the frequency of the need. One scheme which has been suggested as typical for a farmer and his family is as follows:

		Distance
Food necessities } Sweets and tobacco	Village/small town	3–8 miles
Household goods } Working clothes	Small town	10 miles
Children's clothing	Large town	10–30 miles
Better clothing	Larger town	15–30 miles
Display clothing } Better furniture	Provincial centre	50–100 miles
Expensive jewellery	City	100–150 miles

Given an even spread of population, theoretically there should be an even spread of small towns, interspersed with fewer large towns and the occasional city. This pattern breaks down because of the uneven quality of population distribution in all countries, but allowing for this, in Great Britain, for example, these grades of services can be calculated and a so-called 'hierarchy' of towns established. A considerable contribution in this direction has been made by Professor Arthur Smailes,[1] who defines and classifies towns by their functions, from the marginal case which is half town and half village to the complete city. Above I emphasized the shopping needs of families, but a moment's thought will show that other needs are also catered for to different degrees according to a

[1] A. E. Smailes, 'The Urban Hierarchy in England and Wales', *Geography*, XXIX, 1944.

town's place in the hierarchy. For example, primary schools must have as overall a distribution as people, for they must be fairly accessible to everyone. Secondary schools are less frequent, and children must travel farther to them; secondary schools become indices for large towns. Colleges and universities are fewer still, and more scattered. Similarly a local centre will have its doctor and clinic, the larger town its general hospital, the city its specialized clinics and teaching hospitals. The significance of this grading will appear again later, when we deal with the region which a town serves. The emphasis here is on the comparatively regular steps which become apparent in the functions of towns, and that this can be one way of grading and classifying them.

In addition to serving the needs of those who buy goods of all kinds, daily, weekly, or only occasionally—and the term 'market town' exemplifies those which do little else—most towns carry out other important functions, and classifying these has proved quite a difficult task. To the layman it may seem that this is much ado about nothing. You don't need a university education to decide that Crewe is a 'railway town' or that the Rhondda is a 'mining valley', that Birmingham is a 'manufacturing centre', or that Bournemouth is a 'seaside resort'. But this is not the whole story. To a north Cardiganshire farmer Aberystwyth is a market town; to a grammar-school boy from South Wales it is a university town; to a Midlands businessman it is a summer resort. Moreover, once you go beyond the extremely broad generalizations which cover the obvious examples, it becomes apparent that even the tools of description have to be sharpened very considerably.

We can agree that the function of a town, and therefore its classification, should be measured by the jobs people do, rather than, for example, the value of what they produce. So the problem is how to measure the activity of greatest relative importance. The difficulty has already been noted: in addition to specializing in some one thing, all towns are also multi-functional. However obviously the Rhondda Valley spells coal-mining, it could not function unless a very large number of people were shopkeepers, bus drivers, teachers, clerks, postmen, dustmen. As the table overleaf shows, only about 41% of the total employed work in mining; about 20% are employed in manufacturing, another 21% in services, a further 11% in administration. The contrasting figures for Oxford, which do not include students, will be discussed below.

This means that any figure chosen to isolate the special function of a town must to a certain degree be arbitrary. For example, ac-

	Rhondda		Oxford	
Occupations (1961)	No.	%	No.	%
Mining	13,688	41	207	—
Manufacturing	7,106	20	23,663	37
Building	1,161	3	3,509	6
Services	7,171	21	16,333	25
Professional and administration	3,912	11	14,722	23
Miscellaneous	1,701	5	5,641	8
Total	32,283		60,678	

cording to C. D. Harris,[1] a city in the U.S.A. can be classified as a 'wholesale city' when the number employed in wholesaling is at least 20% of the total employed in manufacturing, retail, and wholesale, and at least 45% of the number employed in retail. Or again, 15% or more in mining is enough to classify a town as a mining town, and an educational town qualifies if the college enrolment is 25% or more of the total employed. These examples are enough to illustrate the difficulties and to show the degree of arbitrariness used to bring order into this mass of data. On the basis of such formulae Harris classified the towns and cities of the U.S.A. into nine groups: (a) manufacturing, (b) retail, (c) diversified, (d) wholesale, (e) transport, (f) mining, (g) educational, (h) resorts, (i) others (this includes political). The same criteria could be applied to the towns of Britain, producing a 'common-sense' classification which would be familiar to everyone.

This kind of classification has one serious drawback. Having defined the pigeon-holes, a town can be placed into only one of them. But some towns have many functions. In the United States many of the smaller towns of the high plains are classed as educational centres. A state university certainly dominates even a medium-size town, and this exactly states the function of such a town. But the greater universities, like those of Chicago, Pittsburgh, New York, make no impression at all on their respective cities. In Britain St. Andrews would certainly emerge as a university town, but the very much larger university of Glasgow would disappear without trace in the many functions of that great port. This is to be expected. Maps of cities classified by function should not be read as the distribution of these functions, otherwise the impression would be totally false, but merely of the functions individual towns are mainly

[1] 'A Functional Classification of Cities in the United States', *Geographical Review*, XXXIII, 1943.

concerned with. London is at once the greatest industrial, transport, wholesale and retail, educational, and political centre in the British Isles, and one could take exception to any category it was placed in.

To some extent this can be avoided. Another classification of American cities was made by H. J. Nelson[1] which recognized much the same major classes of economic activities as Harris. They were (a) mining, (b) manufacturing, (c) transport and communications, (d) wholesale, (e) retail, (f) finance, (g) personal, (h) professional, (i) public administration. Dealing with 847 cities (all those of 10,000 population and above) Nelson found the mean percentage for all towns for each of the nine activities, then calculated the standard deviation. Cities with more than 1 SD in any activity were classified according to that activity. Mf 1 meant 1 SD in manufacturing. The degree to which manufacturing dominated was measured by the number of SD's, which was added to the designation—e.g. Mf 2 or Mf 3. But it was also possible to show more than one function. A city might have above 1 SD in manufacturing and in professional; this gave the designation of Mf 1 Pr 1. This is a useful way of recognizing that these classes of activities are not mutually exclusive, and to acknowledge two or more major activities in a town is often much nearer the truth than a statistically correct single-function category. Those who see Oxford as a manufacturing centre and those who prefer to see it as a university town could come to terms in this type of classification, for although the percentage in manufacturing is very high (37%), those engaged in services (25%) and in professional activities (23%) together emphasize its other function, apart from the number of university students who are not included in the employment figures (p. 90).

Both these methods of classification are based on occupations. Not only is this information easily accessible and easily dealt with, but it seems a very reasonable and basic criterion: a town's economic activity is its mainspring. But a piece of machinery is more than a spring, and a town is more than what a town does for its living. Is it possible to quantify these other features and include them as criteria for classification? The data are certainly available. Size is one, density another, age a third. Even more important is the structure of the society: its sex ratio, its age, and its social class. The amount of information which is available in Britain through census data alone is enormous. The problem is how to handle this informa-

[1] 'A Service Classification of American Cities', *Economic Geography*, XXXI, 1955.

tion to produce a classification which will take account of the urban environment and the structure of society. Moser and Scott have classified towns of over 50,000 people in England and Wales, using fifty-seven criteria. The number of permutations is, of course, nearly incomprehensible, and this was a job for a large computer. It was found immediately that the number of criteria could be dramatically reduced because of the high correlation between so many of them. We can expect an industrial town which grew mainly in the second half of the last century to have high densities, that the majority of houses are now sub-standard, that a very high proportion of the people are in the lower socio-economic classes, that families are large and the population young, and that the majority are likely to vote Labour in a parliamentary election.

In some cases the resulting classification is so obvious that the layman may be excused if he decides to dispense with a computer. But the point is, not only that some of the classes are more subtle and refined than those previously used, but that they have been arrived at by using all the relevant data. Even if we fall back on the single criterion of occupation, it is useful to appreciate how many aspects of town life this reflects; and it will certainly be necessary to refine the geographer's tools considerably to bring in aspects other than occupation.

6
The City and the Region

(i)

THE CITY HAS always been inextricably bound up with its surrounding region. Economically and politically there was no dividing line in the Greek city state between the town itself and the countryside around. The distinction, physically accentuated by a wall which made the core of the state a citadel, dissolved before the intimate connexions existing between the town-dwellers and the food-producers. This was a symbiotic relationship. The traders, administrators, craftsmen, teachers lived on the surplus which the land produced, and in exchange they served a large farming community. The economic dependence of towns on the countryside is a basic and constant fact in their existence, though social and political interdependence has varied very considerably at different times in the history of the town. In the Greek *polis* it was very strong.

These regional relationships are implicit in those theoretical networks of towns which have already been discussed and of which Christaller's is the most striking. His hexagons define regions upon which the towns are dependent and which, in turn, depend on those towns for vital services. The smallest scale on which the town-country relationship is clearly illustrated is that of the market town. The market is a focus of farming activity over a well-defined local area. In medieval times the size of the local market and its influence were determined by how many farmers were within easy reach. A visit to market entailed walking there and back within the day, probably with either a burden of produce or herds of cattle or sheep. This meant that farmers rarely came from farther than 3 or 4 miles. The distribution of market towns in England in late medieval times shows that they were usually spaced at intervals of approximately

6 miles. It was illegal to establish a new market within $6\frac{2}{3}$ miles of an existing one. In areas where productivity was low and the population more sparse the distance between markets was considerably greater than this; but generally speaking the region which looked to any one market was small, constricted by the difficulty of travelling. Many of these market towns still remain closely spaced, for although larger towns may have taken over some of their functions, that of marketing local produce is still important, and the farmer's wife, certainly, wants to be within easy reach of some of the more frequent necessities of life. Today a market region with a radius of 10 or 15 miles is quite usual, because travelling is easier. This strictly local dependence which was such a strong medieval element tended to break down when some towns grew at the expense of others. At the other end of the scale the resources of a much wider area focused on a single town could make that town supreme. For example, from late medieval times the rich resources of the whole of the south-east of England were being poured into London. The early growth of Paris can be related to the wealth of the Paris basin. In both cases the wealth of resources played a very large part in the dominance of the capital city over the whole of the state.

(ii)

What links do towns have with their regions today, and how are they measured? In the first instance the purely environmental links should not be forgotten. The city or town has a specific locality, or site, and must come to terms with it. The terrain in the immediate vicinity of a city may play a part in its growth or its form. The altitude of a service reservoir, which restricts the distribution of water to a certain height, may limit the upward expansion of a city. Water is one of those services which can rarely be supplied within a city but which is a vital resource. Without water no city can live. In the Western world the demand for water has increased a hundredfold more than the increase of urban population, and to satisfy it most cities have to look well outside their boundaries. Belfast provides an example of a growing industrial city's search for water in the last 150 years. Up to the end of the 18th century the strictly local supplies of river water and springs were tolerated, though at times there were critical shortages, and as the rivers became polluted the problem was aggravated. By the mid-19th century improved methods of piping and storing were making better use of local resources, but the main source was already outside the town boundary. In the latter part of the 19th century resources in the Antrim plateau, about ten miles outside the boundary, were being used. At the turn of the century it was obvious that the search must be taken still farther, and the tapping of Lough Neagh was seriously considered and only abandoned because of the high cost of pumping water from this very low-lying lake. In 1893 an Act was at last passed which enabled the city to use water from the Mourne Mountains, and in 1901 a 35-mile conduit was opened from this catchment area to the city. In a very real sense the life of Belfast depends on water carried through this conduit.

The larger the city the farther it may have to seek its water. The Welsh mountains supply water to both Birmingham and Liverpool. London finds its water, both from surface and underground sources, in fairly close proximity, but any expansion of London in the metropolitan region would raise the demand enormously, and this is a critical factor for the future. Schemes are being tentatively suggested for the transference of water supplies from one part of the region to another. In the meantime there are plans to tap the water-table itself, and underground water will be piped into the Thames whenever the level of the river falls.

The story is repeated in the New World. By 1900 New York was forced to bring water from the Catskills, 100 miles away. Los Angeles' search for water had to surmount great difficulties. Again the turn of the century saw the search extending beyond the city boundaries, and by 1910 the water of the Columbia River, 150 miles away, was being tapped. This area was put under the jurisdiction of the water authority and by 1913 an aqueduct was bringing the water to the city. This had a curious effect on the growth of Los Angeles and even on the pattern of growth. Obtaining water from such a distance was a vast undertaking which needed great capital expenditure. The townships around Los Angeles could not contemplate such steps and so did the next best thing by asking to be annexed to the city. Los Angeles is a complex of cities whose common need for water has tied them together.

(iii)

The need for water is an example of the environmental link which ties town and country. The resources of a region are another example. In a way the wealth of a region finds its expression in the town or city. Here the resources are built up into the capital without which the life of the city would be meaningless. In all this a measure of control is implicit, and the relationship between town and country is most obviously expressed by administrative links. The overriding fact about the Greek *polis* was its political unity. In Europe the Romans recognized certain areas of land—usually tribal areas—which they called *civitates* long before a town was erected; the town became a focus of an area which had existing ties within it. In medieval times ecclesiastical districts were often based on this more ancient framework, and as the central town then became the seat of a bishop the term *civitas* was transferred from the region to the town, eventually being restricted to the latter. The administrative area preceded the town. This ecclesiastical link in the early medieval period was all-important, and it was only gradually that other functions became associated with it.

Later, civil divisions also stressed the relationship between administrative boundaries and towns. The counties of Midland England all have their shire towns in the centre, and because to some extent communications affected their size, the boundary is approximately a day's journey on horseback away from the town. The system was later copied when the Welsh shires were formed. The duties of the 'shire reeve', or sheriff, have diminished almost to vanishing point, but it was once an important administrative office with responsibility for a compact region focused on the shire town.

Up to 1834 in England the county and the parish—the smallest ecclesiastical division—were the only administrative units that existed, but at that date Poor Law Unions were formed. These were again focused on market towns, where consequently Poor Law Institutions were built. When rural districts were introduced in the 1870s they were based mainly on the Poor Law Unions. The present local authority administrative areas—county borough, urban and rural district—have all to a greater or lesser degree linked a central town with a region around it. Today their relevance to former social and economic factors is all but forgotten. Urban functions have increased, social needs have altered, transport has made sport of distance; even the revision of boundaries is hardly realistic in a rapidly changing society. Today we are more conscious of economic and social forces than we are of administrative areas, and although county loyalties can still be very powerful, such attachments are only sentimental and they rarely dictate our comings and goings.

Of all the regions associated with towns the administrative region is the only one which is clearly defined. However irrelevant they are to everyday life, our municipal and county boundaries are mapped precisely, even if they are sanctioned by nothing more than historical inertia. The real city region is a much more complex and subtle entity, made up of the entire range of diverse activities that link town and country. When we try to define this region, therefore, we are forced to invent methods of measuring the attraction of a town or city in terms of its many functions. I have referred to the city region. To some this suggests relationships too complex to be measured, and other terms have been used to describe the area of interaction. The word *'umland'* has been widely used by German and Scandinavian geographers; 'hinterland' has been used more specifically for areas served by ports; 'catchment area' emphasizes the channelling of people from a wide region towards one point; and 'sphere of influence' suggests the predominance of the town over the country. Professor Smailes has coined the term 'urban field' to emphasize the extent of the attraction of the town. The parallel is with a magnetic field, and where the influence ceases to be felt, people no longer move to that particular pole of attraction, but away from it and towards the next. The advantage of using a term like 'urban field' is that it enables us to reserve the term 'city region' for a similar situation on a much larger scale.

One primary concern of urban geographers has been to delimit urban fields. This involves measuring a town's influence, rarely a simple task. Some criteria of measurement are obvious. The catchment area of a secondary school is one index of the urban field of a large market town, and can be shown simply by plotting the homes of all the pupils who attend that school. A line embracing all these points shows the extent of this particular attraction. Other simple indices include the area over which wholesalers in the town distribute their goods, or how far the delivery service extends from any large store. One useful index is the sales area of an evening or weekly newspaper. Even simpler is the method of plotting the localities which have local items in the paper. Generally speaking, what is being measured is the flow of goods, of people, and of ideas. Around every town and at varying distances from it there are several points where this flow changes direction. These points are, naturally, on lines of movement. Up to this point people look towards town X for their goods and services; beyond this it is easier to turn to town Y. On all lines drawn from town X to all other towns around it, there is such a point. If these are connected they, too, will give us the urban field. This is the basis of Christaller's hypothetical hexagons.

Some geographers have suggested that, as we are measuring movement—and the direction of movement—the influence of

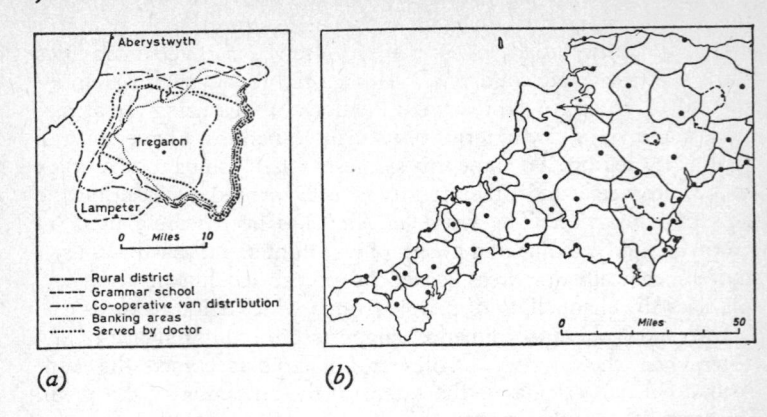

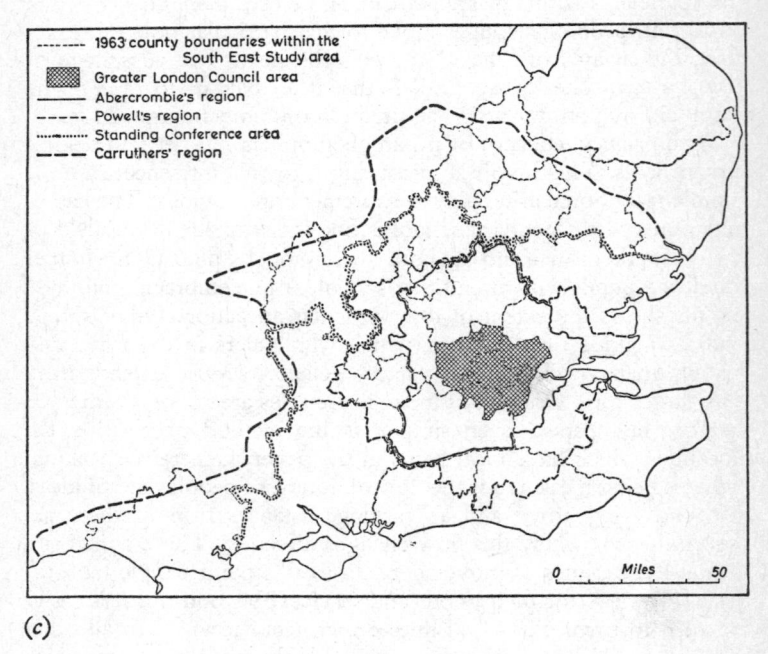

11. *Regions of influence: (a) market town criteria (Wales); (b) local bus service regions (Cornwall); (c) London regions*

towns can be most easily measured by means of bus frequencies. The frequency of buses diminishes as you go away from a town until you reach a point where it is easier to take a bus to the town in an opposite direction. These frequencies are easy to measure, and on this basis the whole of England and Wales has been divided into bus catchment areas[1] which are meant to show the extent of the influence of market towns (Fig. 11b). The method has much to commend it but it also has its shortcomings. It measures public transport only. The use of cars has given the vast majority of people a much greater freedom and range of travel, but this is almost impossible to measure. Another weakness is the assumption that this index is a measure of real areal differentiation, i.e., that the pattern of movement reflects a pre-existing social pattern. It could, of course, be entirely the reverse: that much of the present-day social pattern has been fitted into the most convenient pattern of movement. Membership of a club or an evening class may depend entirely on the bus timetables, and a considerable social change is necessary before this can be altered to meet a new need. Lastly, this is a technique which has been applied only to movements into market towns. In Britain it reveals an overall pattern of fairly small marketing regions, and the activities which are tied in with this are limited to the market-town level.

Even on this level the many links between country and town tend to produce many regions which do not exactly coincide. Although the example chosen here is a very small market town (Tregaron, Cardiganshire), it illustrates this point (Fig. 11a). Only five criteria were chosen, administrative, educational, retail trade, banking, and medical service. Four of these coincide on the east where the county boundary runs along a high plateau edge. All the farms to the west of this line are served by Tregaron; but the limit of food distribution by co-operative store vans which coincides with the area of more dense settlement is a more realistic line. There is a fair coincidence of limits on the sparsely populated coastal plateau between Tregaron and the sea, although the co-operative store serves part of the coast as well. There is considerable discrepancy in the south, for whereas Lampeter—a much larger market town— offers a variety of shops, banks, and doctors, it has no grammar school. The map shows that there is, without doubt, a large area of about 150 square miles which looks to Tregaron for its services; but it would take a bold man confidently to draw a single line around

[1] F. H. W. Green, 'Urban Hinterlands of England and Wales', *Geographical Journal*, CXVI, 1950.

this region when these five services vary so much. In fact the variation would not increase greatly if there were a dozen criteria, but it does emphasize the give-and-take at the periphery of an urban field. One can either generalize for several criteria and use one line, or make a case for one criterion, which will represent the total economic and social activity of the region. The map of bus services discussed above does the latter.

It was pointed out earlier that just as there seems to be a grading of towns by size and function, so there is a grading of urban fields. Tregaron is a small town at the lowest grade of activity. The people of the Tregaron region, and of half a dozen similar ones in west Wales, go to Aberystwyth for better shopping, for a cinema show, or for hospital treatment, because for these services they are within the latter's influence. For still better shopping and an occasional theatre visit they will probably go to Swansea. Many of them visit London on special occasions. These are widening areas of influence. If Green had extended his studies to long-distance express bus services he would have had a map of a few very large regions centred on the large cities. This grading outwards of influence is particularly true of the bigger city, whose widest influence is that of its most specialized function. If the small market town is at one end of the scale, at the other is the large city which, in Britain, provides almost all our needs. As far as influence is concerned our large cities have carved up the whole country between them, because there is no place so remote that it does not at some time or other have to look to a major city for some of its needs. Anglesey is an example. Its links with Liverpool are good, the 90-mile journey is relatively fast by rail and road. Although it has its own local weekly papers in addition to the national dailies, one of the most influential newspapers in the island is the *Liverpool Post*. For luxury shopping, for good-class furniture and clothes, Liverpool is its metropolis. A serious illness calls for a visit to a Rodney Street specialist; and for medical treatment, a nursing-home or hospital bed in Liverpool is first choice—there is even a good chance that the nurses can speak Welsh. Before nationalization it was the Merseyside Electricity Board which lit the Celtic twilight of Anglesey. Compared with Liverpool the towns of South Wales are another and an almost inaccessible world. Liverpool's influence in South Lancashire and Cheshire is obvious, its influence over North Wales more subtle, but still very strong.

Cities with regions of influence similar to that of Liverpool include Newcastle, Leeds, Birmingham, Bristol, Manchester, Belfast.

The last is a city whose region coincides with the state of Northern Ireland, for with a population of about half a million it is ten times as large as Londonderry, the next largest town. Economically and culturally Belfast dominates the country. The others can be called regional capitals, though it is likely that in addition there would be smaller towns like Norwich, Cambridge, Oxford, and Plymouth which would serve areas of less population. It would be true to say, however, that all these regions could be called city regions.

The larger of these city regions are on a par with the metropolitan regions of the United States. These latter are the areas dominated by metropolitan cities which, in their range of services and goods, can satisfy most of the needs of vast sections of the countryside. They, again, have been measured in terms of marketing and trade areas, and of newspaper circulation. They vary in size according to the density of population, the largest being in the plains and in the west and the smallest in the megalopolis of the north-eastern seaboard. But no area lies outside them. There is a sense in which everyone in the Western world is urbanized and is in some degree dependent on a city.

(iv)

In all these cases geographers have delimited the regions. What meaning do these lines have? To what extent are they academic exercises and to what extent do they express real conditions? At best they are a simplification of very complex relationships which do not necessarily have identical distributions. Most of them are based on movements of goods and stress the economic dominance of the city—as, for example, the extent of market influence. But within this wide area the grip of the city tightens as you move nearer the centre and it dominates more and more aspects of life; whereas more diffuse influences, particularly ideas and trends, will probably spread far beyond the economic sphere of influence. The regional boundary is only an attempt to show where the critical changes occur. There is something to be said for substituting a series of zones. If this were done for many cities the result would be extremely confusing, but one city only will illustrate how complex its varying influence may be. London is a good example (Fig. 11c).

If the whole of Britain is divided into city regions, then London is reduced to the same status as Birmingham, Manchester, or Liverpool, sometimes referred to as 'second-order' cities. We are comparing those functions in London which match the provincial cities, and setting on one side those that make London pre-eminent in the entire country. The administrative region of London is very small indeed. Between 1888 and 1965 it was the County of London. However much people in the south-east of England as a whole looked to London, administrative control was restricted to this central area. By 1965 the county was even an administrative anomaly, for it covered less than a third of a built-up area whose administration was shared by Middlesex, Essex, Kent, and Surrey. This was eventually recognized by the creation of the Greater London Authority, whose administrative boundary ran through the green belt, and therefore encompassed the conurbation, incidentally swallowing the whole of Middlesex and parts of Surrey, Kent, and Essex. How realistic is this? Twenty years earlier Abercrombie was advocating a planning region extending far beyond this, absorbing Surrey, much of Kent and Essex, and much of Hertfordshire and Buckinghamshire. Nothing could better illustrate London's influence in this 'country zone' outside the green belt than the creation of eight satellite towns to take its expanding population. But even Abercrombie's region ceased to be realistic to planners, and in 1960 the Ministry of Housing and Local Government suggested a Metropolitan Region which extended to Brighton in the south, included Reading in the west, and touched Cambridgeshire in the north. Geographers were critical of this region again because it was too restricted. Why cut off eastern Kent and the East Sussex coast? Where did they belong if not to London? And surely West Sussex and the remainder of Essex have commuter links with London which are increasing rapidly? In other words, population changes and movements suggest a more rectangular region, much nearer the 'second-order' region with which we began. The London city region is, in effect, this, with the exception of 'third-order' regions around Southampton, Oxford, and Cambridge. However strong London's influence is in the south-east it is felt that these three cities have the size and character to be considered separately. To sum up, there is an inner administrative region, a much wider planning region (but with no executive power), and a still wider geographer's region; and it is the latter which links up with other city regions in England and which implies that no area now lies outside the influence of a major city. The critical changes brought about by the growth of London are now taking place in this wider region, and it is a great pity that the administration is so far from catching up with these events. It will probably be overcome only by some system of regional planning administration.

There was a time when the sharp differentiation in function

between town and country—reflected in the abrupt change on either side of the city wall—was mirrored in the social pattern of two societies, however interdependent they were. Now this, too, has gone. Rapid movement has put the countryside within the city-dwellers' reach: remote hamlets and sleepy villages harbour stockbrokers and company directors. Even more important, wireless and television are bringing the city within reach of the countryman himself. This is why the reality of the city region is increasing and why its administrative recognition is long overdue.

7
Man and the City

(i)

ABOVE ALL ELSE a city is a living thing. Much of the analysis and classification of the preceding chapters has dealt with the dry bones only. Structure, form, function, although they all arise from men's activities and consequently reflect them, can be dealt with without reference to society; even though the nearest parallel to this approach may be the anatomist's specimen on a dissecting-table. This is of course a necessary and fundamental way to get nearer to understanding the city in many of its aspects. But it would be a pity if it were left at that. The most vital element in the city is the society which lives in it. The study of urban society has always attracted scholars, and there are many more contributions on this aspect than on the more structural side of the city that I have already dealt with. Perhaps the most interesting problems of all arise where these two approaches meet. Urban societies live and move within a complex of buildings and streets; they help to create it and to a certain degree they reflect it. A city environment is as much a matter of men and women as it is of houses and shops. And within the city distinctive environments are created because the groups and classes which make up the urban society occupy distinctive areas, have different occupations, move differently, and live differently.

Before discussing these differences within it which make a city or town so interesting, we should remember that even as a whole the population of the town is very different from that of the country. Sociologists have measured the difference between urban and rural society in all its aspects, but here we are interested in the major differences only. Everyone is agreed that density is one of the elements which distinguishes the urban from the rural society. Though they vary greatly urban densities are always high. Even in Britain, where densities have been considerably reduced by the open suburban extensions typical of this century, there are few cities in which less than 10,000 people live on every square mile. Edinburgh, for example, has a density of over 9,000 per square mile and Bristol about 10,500. Belfast has 18,500 people to the square mile. In the developing countries the figures are much higher, those of Delhi and Calcutta, for instance, approaching 400,000. These are frightening figures. The densities of British cities are in a way underestimated, for they are gross density figures, i.e., the number of people expressed as a ratio of all the land within a city boundary, including parklands and industrial and shopping areas as well as residential. If the ratio is calculated in terms of residential land only then this figure—the net density—is much higher. If we accept the inter-war standard of suburban density at 12 houses to the acre, and further accept an average of just over 4 persons in each family, this gives a residential density of about 32,000 to the square mile. Even the most dispersed city, therefore, has a very high density, and unless there is the most radical of technical changes in land use, this will continue to be the most obvious distinguishing mark of towns and cities.

Differences in the occupation of the people between town and country have already been implied. Again it is a primary premise that most towns are not concerned with agriculture. The exceptions are the West African towns and some Indian towns, where the percentage of farmers and farm labourers is high enough to make these the dominant occupational class. But on the whole the population of a town is concerned with manufacturing and services in the widest sense. Many of the familiar—if stereotyped—differences between the town-dweller and his country cousin arise from this fact. The entire pattern of town life reflects a severance from the soil and, as a consequence, habits, dress, food, and traditions in general, differ from those of the countryside. If this difference is now decreasing it is because the countryside is being permeated by ideas which originate in the town; the industrial pattern is setting the pace.

Another aspect of contrast which we will deal with in greater detail later is that of the heterogeneity of urban society as opposed to the relative homogeneity of the rural. This is a gross oversimplification, of course, and implies that rural societies are also rather static; this is now continually being shown to be untrue. What is true is that rural society at any one time has a stability, or an equilibrium, which is often derived from its relationship with the land. It is often easy to recognize a rural pattern of culture and appreciate its ecological base. It is popularly thought—and probably over-emphasized—that urban society represents a breakdown of this stability, much of which is linked with family ties. The verse 'Any old place I hang my hat Is home sweet home to me' refers to the absence of ties in the town, and to the social anonymity of the individual. Specialization and differentiation are among the keynotes of urban life. Wirth stressed that this had a great effect on social interaction. The words 'superficial', 'anonymous', 'transitory' occur again and again in studies of city life. Moreover contacts become impersonal as they are multiplied and as they throw together people of diverse interests. As a social order urbanism is characterized by the substitution of secondary for primary contacts. This apparent breaking-down of society into disparate groups arises not only from the multiplicity of roles which town people perform, but also from the fact that the population is derived from elsewhere. Until fairly recently the growth of any city depended on attracting people from the countryside. This may bring not only diversity of *mores*, but even diversity of culture and of race. Our greatest cities have often attracted people from most parts of the world and are cosmopolitan in character.

(ii)

Not only do these elements—density, occupational structure, heterogeneity—differ markedly between town and country, but they differ within towns and cities. In no town is there anything approaching an even spread of population to give an overall density. In Belfast, which is fairly typical of a large industrial city in Britain (it has half a million inhabitants), net density varies from 320 per square mile to 180,000. This may seem more real in terms of acres, for the units from which these densities were calculated are the enumeration districts. These are fairly small, compact bits of the city which have a population of between 1,000 and 2,000—the most convenient unit for a single census enumerator. The range, then, is from 1 person per 2 acres at one extreme in areas of upper-class villas, to 280 persons per acre in the oldest working-class districts where mid-Victorian by-law houses crowd back to back. About a quarter of the population in the better suburbs live at densities of between 0·5 and 38·8 persons per acre (320–25,000 per square mile), and another quarter occupying row houses live at high densities of between 142 and 280 per acre (90,000–180,000 per square mile). Incidentally, the equation between density and standard of living is a fairly straightforward one in Belfast but would not necessarily be so in some cities where there are many flats or apartment houses. In some parts of London the most extreme densities are found in upper-class blocks of flats.

That there are variations in density is apparent to even a casual observer. The question arising in the mind of an urban geographer or ecologist is whether there is a pattern in the variation, and whether this pattern is found in other cities. There is a pattern. It follows closely the kind of use made of the land, and as this itself has a fairly regular pattern in Western cities, it means that we can expect high densities in certain parts of the city, light in another. In the centre the densities are extremely light. This is because there are so few households here. All that the census can register are a few caretakers and those staying at hotels. For the rest the heart of the city is a mass of shops and offices, empty of permanent population. Immediately beyond this centre, where we usually find older houses interspersed with industry, the densities rise very sharply. They fall equally rapidly on the outskirts of the city where the newer—and middle-class—suburbs predominate. Although there are modifications of this simple picture, the generalization stands for most industrial Western cities. Liverpool is an example. The conurbation of Liverpool was defined in 1951, and within it were recognized three major zones: (a) the centre, which included the dock area and most of the business and retail shopping area; (b) beyond the centre, and encircling it, a zone of older residential streets, some middle-class and some industrial; (c) beyond this again a suburban zone, mainly residential. A density map showed that the centre was lightly peopled—with the density in one area as low as 8 persons per acre (5,000 per square mile)—but the second zone had very high densities, predominantly 64–127 per acre (41,000–85,000 per square mile). The suburban zone again was one of light density.

The pattern crops up again in London. However busy the City may be during the day it is very empty at night, and in parts density is as low as 6 to 10 per acre (3,800–6,400 per square mile). Between the inner City and the boundary of the old London County Council the density is consistently above 61 per acre (45,000 per square mile). Between this and the green belt, in the suburban zone, the density is much less, usually varying between 10 and 42 to the acre (6,400–27,000). (These are gross densities, but the contrast is very clear.) This is not to imply that there are always three clear-cut zones—the number may depend on how minutely the problem is being studied. But it does mean that all large cities in Britain have a centre in which densities are very light, followed usually by a zone of high densities; these grade outwards, a more sudden step to light densities being sometimes apparent where terrace houses give way to inter-war semi-detached houses. The variations within these major zones are due to class differences, for, as we have seen, in suburbia itself density varies between 50 or so persons to the acre to 1 person per two acres.

On the other side of the Atlantic a similar density pattern re-emerges, whether in Boston, Chicago, or New York. The New York Metropolitan Area will serve as an example. The density of Manhattan is very high—108,000 per square mile (170 per acre) on intensively developed land; but this figure itself is the mean of the light-density downtown areas and the much more densely peopled areas beyond the central business district. Brooklyn, Queens, and Bronx vary between 25,000 and 55,000 per square mile (40–85 per acre). Beyond this, in what is called the inner ring of counties, it is 9,000 to 16,500 per square mile (14–25 per acre), and farther out still, in the outer ring of counties, it is 1,700 to 7,400 per square mile (3–11 per acre). These figures are closely related to kinds of dwelling-houses, for in Manhattan only 1·8% are single-family dwellings, and 97·4% are apartments; in the remainder of the core (Brooklyn, Queens, and Bronx) there are still only 18·9% single-family dwellings. But in the inner ring of counties the figure is 57·7% and in the outer it is 69·8%.

However accurately the density map is drawn it has one great shortcoming. It is a static picture, and it inevitably suggests a static situation. What a pity that for census purposes we are recorded only when we sleep. The density map is a picture of the city at rest. But movement is the life-blood of a city. This is particularly so since growth and comparative ease of movement have together divorced the two major parts of man's life—his work and his home. In a peasant community workplace and home are one. Even in early industrial cities it was to everyone's advantage that the worker be near the mill, and in all cities before public transport changed the scene walking time limited the distance between home and work. Today the commuter thinks nothing of travelling 25 or even 50 miles to his work. With this increasing dispersal of homes has come the increasing specialization of offices and shops in the centre. Consequently there is a vast daily movement in all great cities, between centre and suburb. A mid-day density map of London looks very different from that drawn from census data. A comparatively modest 28-floor block of offices in Knightsbridge, empty at night, has a day population of 2,500. The Loop area of Chicago, which at night has a population of only 6,000 or so, attracts a million workers every day.

Daily experience of rush-hour travel might convince one that reality is neither the density pattern at midnight nor that at midday; it is, rather, the travelling itself. There is no very adequate technique of illustrating the daily comings and goings in a great city. The journey to work has been the subject of various investigations, and there are figures which give some impression of this great and increasing movement. (In parenthesis we might note that they do not account for all movement, for housewives repeat the inward and outward journeys to a lesser degree for occasional shopping, and evening entertainment, which is concentrated at the centre, pushes the flow well into the night.)

One way in which the journey to work has been measured in London is by calculating the percentage of the occupied night population in each local authority who work in the central area. Around the central area itself the percentage is very high, and even in Finchley and Southgate, about 7 miles north of the centre, in Beckenham, an equal distance to the south-east, and in Purley, 10 miles to the south, the percentage is between 30 and 45. In a very broad belt which can be called the suburbs (part of the conurbation), it varies from up to 20% in the west and north-east, to 20%–30% in the north and south; and the commuting areas of Hertfordshire in the north-west and Sevenoaks in the south-east have up to 20% of their occupied population working in Central London. It is also clear that the higher percentage is found in areas farther from the centre than formerly. In 1921 the percentage who lived in the County of London and worked in the centre was 66; in 1951 it was only 50. The percentage in the inner ring of suburbs increased a little between 1921 and 1951 from 17 to 19, but the greatest change was in the outer part of the conurbation, where the percentage rose from 9 to 21. Beyond the conurbation the percentage rose from 8 to 10. This trend is continuing.

Nothing demonstrates more clearly the growing separation of work and home in the great city. A large proportion of the jobs are in the centre, but the vast majority live in the suburbs. This has also been expressed in terms of job ratios, i.e., the number of the occupied day population per 100 of the occupied night population. If the ratio is 100 in any local authority area, then theoretically every man can live and work within the same borough (an equal number of men moving in and out would, of course, also give a ratio of 100). On this basis most of Central London has a ratio of over 320, and parts of the City are as high as 556. Correspondingly the inner suburbs have ratios between 65 and 80, and the outer suburbs between 30 and 65. Only beyond the green belt is an equilibrium found, and even there Hertfordshire is an exception.

Office work is the great attraction in the centre, and this seems to be not only disproportionately large, but still greatly expanding, in London. In 1962 London had more than ten times the office space of Birmingham or Liverpool or Manchester; and in the preceding decade it had increased by 25%. Considerable efforts are being made to persuade people to move their offices out of London, but they are most reluctant to do so. For mixed motives the central business district still has an overwhelming attraction. Even when the efforts of the Location of Offices Bureau are successful it does no more than persuade some firms to move to the outer part of the conurbation; and many of the office blocks which are thus emptied are rapidly filled by other firms. Present commitments show that office space will continue to increase in London for a long time: jobs will continue to be generated; people will live still farther out; and movement will increase. The emphasis has been on the concentric arrangements of patterns of movement, bringing out most clearly the movement from the periphery to the centre. It would be a mistake to imagine that this is the only, or even the major, one. In 1951 about a million people travelled daily to the central business district, about 160,000 travelled into the district east of the City, and another 260,000 to other districts in the County of London. But the total number travelling to work in London was about 4½ million, and the majority travelled short distances either within their own borough or to adjacent ones. The pattern of movement is not a simple one from the outside to the centre, but a very complex one of lateral movements as well.

One generalization which suggests itself is that the radial movements are much longer than the lateral movements. There is certainly evidence of this from New York, where those who work in Manhattan spend an average of one hour travelling to their work; those working in other core areas within the metropolitan area take between half an hour and three-quarters; those working in the inner belt of counties in the metropolitan area take twenty minutes to half an hour; and those in the outer belt between ten and twenty-five minutes. An interesting result of the fact that higher social classes tend to live in suburban and commuting areas is the different commuting time for various occupational groups. Again in New York a professional man or an executive takes an average of a little over three-quarters of an hour to get to work, compared with thirty-five minutes for a factory worker and twenty-five minutes for those in retail trades. Good access to the job is still much more important for service workers, craftsmen, and labourers than it is for the professional and managerial classes.

So far we have considered the daily movements in a large city, mainly the movement from homes to jobs. There is another sense in which the city-dweller is very mobile, and that is in moving from one house to another. It has already been suggested that the individual—and even the family—is less 'rooted' in a city than in the country. The breakdown of close kinship ties, the substitution of impersonal methods of communication for personal, and the tendency to demonstrate the climb up the economic and social ladder by moving into better houses—all these diminish a sense of belonging to a community and make movement easier. It is difficult to measure this mobility. We know that in the twelve months of 1949 14·7% of the total population of the metropolitan region of New York moved house. This is a high figure, though it has probably increased considerably since then. What is more interesting is its breakdown, for although mobility was high in Manhattan (13·3%) it was low elsewhere in the city, only to rise again very considerably in the inner ring of counties, and it was as high as 26·8% in parts of the outer counties. The last figure is easily understood because it represents many who moved into the area for the first time as new houses were continually being built.

Another way of estimating movement is to measure population change over a period of years. This will show those areas losing population and those gaining; though we should remember that the net figure probably hides very considerable movement and also includes the natural increases and decreases in population due to the differences between birth rates and death rates. But in London, for example, we can look at the pattern of total change, due to all causes, and this shows an overall movement from the centre outwards. The centre of London lost population rapidly between 1951 and 1961. In the centre it is common to find losses of 7% to 14%, and in a few areas the loss is as much as 60%. Outside the central area, the suburbs show generally high increases of up to about 20%. Again we should remind ourselves that natural increase would account for between 2% and 10%, but the gain is nevertheless considerable. Peripherally the increases are even greater, in places amounting to over 40%. The overall impression is of the emptying of the centre and the piling up of population around the fringes or the city area. This happens elsewhere. In the twenty years before 1951 Liverpool showed decreases both in the centre (a loss of 3·9%) and in the belt of older houses around this (a loss of 10%—though much of this was undoubtedly the result of destruction during the war). On the other hand the suburban zone showed a massive increase of 104%.

To complete the story of London's moving population we must go beyond the conurbation and even the green belt. Since 1945 the L.C.C. have settled about 200,000 people in housing estates lying outside the county, and a further 300,000 have settled in the eight new towns which lie outside the green belt at an average distance of about 20 miles. In addition 200,000 people have moved into towns which are expanding by agreement with the planning authorities, some of them as far away as 40 miles. The latest study of the possible distribution changes of the next twenty years suggests cities and towns at an average of 50 miles away from London, and although this is a measure to cope with the population increase of the entire south-east region, there is no doubt at all that it is no more than a reflection of the attraction and growth of London, and an extension of the peripheral growth which has characterized the metropolitan region for the last century or more.

The general patterns of density, of daily movement, and of changes in population discussed so far are common to most larger Western cities. The pre-industrial city presents a very different picture, though there is often a paucity of data to substantiate the more subjective impressions. High overall densities have already been mentioned, though the difficulty of comparing these with densities in Western cities is increased by the comparative uniformity of types of building throughout: the small single-family dwelling is as common in the centre as on the outskirts. High density therefore commonly means overcrowding. This undifferentiated nature of the city is particularly true in the towns of Nigeria, where density may be around 21,000 per square mile. This is approximately 33 per acre, but if this sounds light we must remember that, in the absence of open spaces and amenities, the gross density approaches the net density. It is also unlikely to vary to any degree within the town, whether near the centre or near the outskirts. Much higher densities are found in the more advanced pre-industrial cities and here, too, there is a little less uniformity. Most of these cities are crowded at their centre. The heart of Rangoon has densities up to

200,000 per square mile (300 per acre gross), and parts of Delhi and Calcutta have double this number. Even in these cities residential and business functions have not yet been separated. The shopping street combines house and shop, and the workshop is often nothing more than floor-space in, or attached to, the house. The crowded centre is, then, typical, as well as the uniform density beyond. It follows that the change from urban to rural on the outskirts is very sharp, and this is certainly reflected in densities. In Bombay, after a very narrow suburban zone, the densities drop from the uniform 20,000 per square mile (31 per acre) to a rural density of 250 (less than 1 per 2 acres). The only exceptions are along radial roads, where near-urban densities persist up to the periphery of the wider metropolitan area. This very sharp grading—which is reflected in so many urban features—is typical of the pre-industrial city (Delhi, Madras, Hyderabad, Calcutta, and Baroda all show the same pattern) and so is the completeness of the change from urban to rural immediately beyond the built-up area: within the dense belts of these cities 94% or more people are in non-agricultural occupations, whereas immediately beyond the percentage drops to 10%.

In pre-industrial cities the problem of the journey to work has nowhere reached the proportion that it has in Western cities. There are still many people who live on the same premises where they work, but with the increase in service industries, the development of a central business district, and the physical growth of cities, the amount of movement is increasing very considerably; though in many cities it is confined to movement on foot or by bicycle. Nor can residential changes be compared with those in Western cities. Traditionally the centre of the city is a place shared by the upper and lower classes. Even professional men may live near their work. More recently, movement outwards has followed the Western pattern. In Rangoon some of the *élite* have moved out and built houses around the golf course, race track, and university. This has little effect on the outskirts generally because here—as in many of these cities—the outer belt is mainly one of densely populated shacks built by squatters. But it does show a move towards the Western pattern.

(iii)

Density, mobility, and changes reflect the whole society. We must now consider some of the different elements in society and the way in which these vary both between town and country and within different parts of the town. The most fundamental is the ratio of women to men. In Western countries it is usually the case that in towns there is a higher ratio of women to men than one would expect, and consequently in country districts the ratio is lower than normal. This is certainly so in the British Isles. Generally speaking the departure from the normal balance is not very startling, but over the whole country certain differences do stand out. Rural Ireland has a much lower than normal ratio of between 85 and 95 women per 100 men, contrasting strongly with Dublin's ratio of 115 to 125. The midland valley of Scotland tends to have high ratios (105–125), and so does the south-east of England, but the very high ratios, i.e., over 125, are in towns and cities. More particularly are they found in coastal resorts: along the south coast Lyme Regis, Bournemouth, Ventnor, Worthing, Hove, Brighton, Eastbourne, and Hastings are all in this category; so are Herne Bay, Margate, Ramsgate, and Clacton; in the north, Whitby, Scarborough, and Bridlington, and Morecambe, St. Annes, and Southport; in Wales, Conway, Llandudno, Colwyn Bay, and Rhyl; and in Scotland, Saltcoats and Ayr. This phenomenon is even evident in Northern Ireland, where Newcastle, Ballycastle, and Portrush are in this category, and in the Republic, Dun Laoghaire. The only inland towns with comparable figures are Harrogate, Windermere, and Ambleside. The need for women in services in such resorts must be added to the fact that many women also retire there, and as they live longer than men and consequently outnumber them considerably in the older age groups, this has a marked effect on the entire population structure. But it only accentuates the fact that the proportion of women in towns is consistently higher than it is in the countryside.

The accompanying table shows the ratio of women to men in towns for a number of Western countries, some Latin American

Females per 100 males in towns of over 20,000 inhabitants (1950)

Finland	123	Nicaragua	130	Japan	103
Austria	123	Dominican Rep.	117	Turkey	93
Switzerland	117	Chile	117	India	86
France	116	Brazil	109	Ceylon	78
W. Germany	113	Argentina	103	N. Borneo	78
Spain	111	Venezuela	101	Pakistan	75
England & Wales	109				
New Zealand	107			Egypt	98
United States	106				
Canada	104				

countries, and some Asian. At first glance it is tempting to correlate these figures with degree of urbanization, which is certainly very high in most countries in the first group, still relatively high in the second, although they are so-called developing countries, and low in the third. This would be too simple an equation, however, as the ratios reflect the entire social and economic structure of these countries. The main contrast is between the African and Asian countries and the remainder of the world. The pattern of the latter is familiar, and in addition to what has already been said above it should be added that women migrate to towns to work in light industries. It is significant that Japan is the only exception in the Asian group and approximates to the Western pattern largely for this last reason. Otherwise the Asian figures reflect the migrant labour of these countries, which is almost entirely male. The women stay at home. This, then, is mainly a regional pattern, which also indicates that urbanization in Asia often leads to an upset in the balance of men and women. There are some indications that it may be changing. In Rangoon, for example, the ratio was as low as 48 in 1931, but by 1950 it was 86. It is quite obvious that the gross disparity of a figure like 48 cannot be maintained for long. It represents the first massive intake of male labour, but as these men marry many bring their wives back with them. With population growth the situation tends gradually to right itself until it is relatively stable. This may mean that Asian cities may be approaching more nearly to the Western pattern (as Japan has done), but this will entail a fairly radical change in outlook and particularly in the status of women. The very slight data on China suggest a similar picture. In Kunming, a city of half a million people in south-west China, the ratio was 78 in the city itself and 92 in the suburbs; but outside the city the ratio varied in rural districts from 104 near the city to 109 away from the city. This suggests that it is tied up with degrees of urban-ness, but the total picture is of predominance of men in the city. Woman's place is in the home, and home is often a farm; in the earlier stages of migration to the city the husband leaves his wife behind. In a curious way, although belonging to the city, he considers his closest ties to be with the countryside he has left.

Sex ratio is only one of many features which show significant contrasts between town and country. This alone would be sufficient to influence the total demographic structure, but in addition there are many other contrasts. For example, infantile mortality is relatively lower in cities compared with the countryside. In England and

Wales the infantile mortality is 29·9 per thousand, but in London it is 26. Similarly, in New York it is 25 compared with 29·2 for the entire United States, 37 in Paris and 52 in France, 27 in Oslo and 28·2 in Norway. In Tokyo the figure is 42 and in Japan it is 60·1. A similar disparity is found in Latin America, though the figures are sometimes much higher: for instance, Buenos Aires' 37 compares with Argentina's 68·2. No figures are available which would permit such a comparison in Africa and Asia, largely because the registration of births, particularly in rural areas, cannot be relied upon. But it is almost certain that the reverse is true and that infantile mortality is higher in towns than it is in rural areas. This was certainly so in Western European cities until comparatively recently. The dramatic decline in infantile mortality has been the result of medical discoveries, and as these were made and applied first in cities the change has taken place here much more rapidly than elsewhere.

Although decline in infantile mortality is probably the greatest factor in increasing the population, this does not necessarily mean that city populations reproduce themselves rapidly, for urbanization, in Western cities particularly, seems to have changed the entire attitude towards family size, and the urban family is smaller than the rural. The fertility ratio, i.e., the number of children under five per 1,000 women between fifteen and forty-nine, is always lower in cities. Whereas for England and Wales the fertility ratio is 32·1, for London it is 29·3; for New York it is 29·7, compared with 41·7 for the United States, and for Copenhagen 28·9, compared with 39·3 for Denmark. In Argentina, too, for Buenos Aires it is 22·0, compared with 42·3 for the country as a whole, and for Mexico City 36·9, compared with 58·0 for Mexico. Even Bombay has a smaller figure (51·6) than that for India as a whole (62·1), but generally speaking the difference is much less in Asian cities. Here—and to a lesser extent in some Latin American cities—it is because the influx of so many peasants brings with it rural *mores*. The reverse is true in Britain, where the balance may well be approached from the opposite direction, by urban standards becoming gradually accepted in the countryside.

Age differences are particularly interesting, more particularly within cities. In Western cities there is no great difference between the distribution of age groups in urban and rural areas, but there can be quite considerable differences between one city and another. It is obvious, for example, that in a south coast resort the number of old people is relatively high and the number of children consequently low. In the United States a study has been made of the relative size of age groups in cities of 25,000 people and over. Many of these cities approximate very closely to the average national pattern, but others deviate from this very considerably. Those cities which are still growing rapidly by attracting people from elsewhere, like Washington and Houston, are heavy in the productive ages, but have relatively few children and old people. Cities in pleasant areas which attract retired folk—Pasadena, and in Florida—are very top-heavy in the older age groups, while university towns such as Berkeley, Cambridge, and Madison show a great concentration in the 18–30 age groups. Many cities, including Boston, show an old and young predominance, because they have grown in two phases, after the First World War and after the Second; whereas others which have settled down after a period of growth between the wars show a high proportion of middle-aged persons. Some of these patterns are due to the growth structure of the city, but most of them are affected by migration. Cities owe so much to the populations which they absorb that they tend to reflect the migrant characteristics. This is true in our own new towns. In 1961, compared with the age-grouping of Britain as a whole, new towns had comparatively few older people, a marked peak of population between 35–50, and another marked peak under 15 years of age. The first peak is of those people who moved into these towns over the last fifteen years, and they were mainly young. They were the child-producing group and consequently the second peak is equally marked.

Normal age-group patterns are particularly disturbed in pre-industrial cities in Asia. Generally speaking many towns show fewer people in the older categories and in the younger. But this may be exaggerated by the male migrants, who swell the 15–45 age groups quite disproportionately. Compared with the average, the 'excess' men in this category account for 13·5% of the total population of Calcutta, a gross imbalance which is commonly found. This imbalance is not found to the same extent in the developing countries of Latin America. Here the age and sex balance in cities is fairly normal. This may be very surprising considering the great and continuous drift of rural migrants into all the major cities, but this is a drift not of male workers only, but of families. The intake is normally structured and has no effect on the total picture.

Within the Western city the varieties of age-group structures are very interesting. Belfast shows the complexity of age structure in its different localities (Fig. 12). On the map twenty-two enumeration

12. Age/sex differences within a city (Belfast)

districts have been chosen which illustrate the possible age-group patterns. Here they are combined with sex, so that the age groups on the right of each pyramid refer to women and those on the left to men. But as the sex differences are not great, these comments will be confined mainly to the age classes which are in five-year groups (0–5, 6–10, 11–15, 16–20, etc.). Remember that the age/sex pattern for the whole city (1951) is roughly a pyramid with a slightly restricted base and a slight 'middle-age spread'. Near the city centre (enumeration district A on the map) the normal pattern has broken down completely. Apart from the fact that there are few children and that there seem to be a great many men between 20 and 25, it has no rhyme or reason. This is to be expected in an area where there are few houses. The pyramid is that of an hotel population together with a couple of seamen's hostels. Moving to the west of the centre, districts H and I—and particularly the latter—are much more like the average, although H has more children under 15. This is an industrial district of small terraces of 19th-century by-law houses; the standard family unit is almost undisturbed, but the greater number of children is fairly typical of a working-class community. Near-by are districts D and E. These are physically identical: the housing and occupational structures are indistinguishable from those of H and I because they lie in the same industrial zone. But the pyramids are quite markedly different, showing heavy preponderance of adolescents and young children. The only difference between these pairs of districts is that H and I are 95% Protestant and D and E are 95% Roman Catholic. Religious differences will be dealt with below; here it is sufficient to point out that they can have a radical effect on age-group structure. There is a further marked contrast between the last four pyramids and those of U, V, O, and P. The most striking characteristic of these is the large number of older people, the increased 'middle-age spread', and the comparatively small percentage of children. These are all suburban middle-class areas, and can be called 'ageing' localities, a feature emphasized by the number of old people who retire to these suburbs. Again religious differences can introduce a new factor: G, for example, is also a suburb with social and physical characteristics like O and P, but with the difference that it is over 90% Roman Catholic, and consequently the number of children is very much greater. Indeed the suburban middle-class Roman Catholic age-group pattern (G) is similar to the Protestant lower-class pattern (I). Next to G is a Roman Catholic housing estate, and here is an exaggerated version of the pattern of D: the number of grandparents is exceedingly small, that of adolescents and children exceedingly high. Two other pyramids need explaining. Near the centre of the city and adjacent to the university is enumeration district T, characterized by many middle-aged and older persons, a very marked number of younger people between 20 and 30, and comparatively very few children. This is a rooming area and shows the typical characteristics of such areas. Here there are hundreds of students, clerks, and nurses living in lodgings or in flats in terraces of former middle-class houses. Householders who have not moved to smaller houses in modern suburbs have been forced to let part of their houses in rooms—and the pyramid even shows the preponderance of middle-aged and elderly women who are landladies. The second unusual pyramid is J, a post-World War I housing estate. The upper half of this pyramid still shows what its pattern was when it was built—quite similar to that of F. But such housing rarely allows for the expansion which children growing to maturity demand: consequently the over-20s have to move out. More recently the increase in the number of children is showing as a second broadening near the base.

This analysis has shown in fair detail that great variations in age-group structure can be expected within a city. It was complicated by differences introduced by religion, but if we eliminate these for a moment there are certain generalizations which can be suggested. First, there is the lack of pattern at the city centre; secondly, the fairly broad-based pyramid showing a high proportion of children is found in the zone immediately outside the centre; thirdly, the suburban zone on the whole has a mature and old population. This is certainly substantiated in other Western cities. In Liverpool, for example, in the inner section, which includes the older industrial housing, children under 15 accounted for 31% of the population. Outside this the percentage dropped to 23, although on the periphery it rose in places to 30. On the other hand the proportion aged over 55 in the first zone was only 15%, in the second it rose to 20%, dropping to 17% in the outer zone. In London, although class composition is the main determinant in age pattern, nevertheless the dominance of certain classes in certain areas also gives a spatial pattern not unlike that already suggested; and in addition there are differences irrespective of class which show that migration to the outer suburbs is attractive to families with young children. The proportion of children under 15 ranges from under 17% near the centre to 25% in the most recent suburbs. The proportion of old people is sometimes as low as 5% in these outer suburbs, but is high in the well-established suburbs near the centre. The attraction of the centre itself for young people comes out very clearly. In London it can be said that between the inner part and the outer suburbs the age structure is fairly normal. Near the centre there are (a) areas with the disproportionate number of young people but few children (e.g. Paddington), (b) others, such as the boroughs of the East End, with a high proportion of children and a slight excess of young men, and (c) some inner well-established suburbs which show a predominance of elderly people (e.g. Wimbledon). The outer suburbs all have a characteristically high proportion of children, fewer young people than average, and a fairly high proportion in the young parental groups.

Studies have been made of age differences in the zones of the

New York metropolitan district, but it should be remembered that this is a very much wider area than that of the London conurbation. The only significant comparison is that the proportion of children is relatively small in Manhattan—16·7% under 15—but that it rises to 22·1% in the remainder of the city, and a little higher in the commuting inner and outer county zones. The percentage of these over 65 years of age drops from 8·74% in Manhattan to 7·32% in the core area and only rises significantly in the outer county zone.

It is very difficult indeed to generalize, though in each case there is a distinct areal pattern within which differences are very marked. There are major differences between the centre, with its attraction for the single young people, and the outer suburbs, which attract young families. Between the two extremes the stable 'normal' pattern is often upset by the preponderance of one class or another, industrial areas having more children, old-established residential areas having ageing populations. One last point should be stressed, however, and that is the changing nature of these patterns. The centre will always have its attraction for the unattached young, and for a time the established residential area will retain its character; but in most suburbs the population matures, and new growing areas outside the conurbation will take on the characteristics of the young age/sex pyramid.

(iv)

Occupations are among the most diverse aspects of life in a city. We associate the countryside with only a small range of jobs, and consequently with a fairly simple class system. The city is associated with not only the most exalted of occupations and those most divorced from manual labour, those in government, learning, the arts, but also the most menial; and to a large degree class derives from occupation. In Western cities there is relatively free access to all the occupational groups for all people, a great amount of occupational mobility, and consequently considerable class mobility. There are reservations to such a generalized statement, but a sharp contrast is presented by some Eastern cities where the correlation of occupation with caste rather than class restricts mobility and tends to isolate groups by occupation as well as by racial or ethnic origin.

In most Western cities one can isolate occupation from most other kinds of group except that of social class. The correlation between job and class is very marked. In our census social classes are based on groupings of occupations, and those cases where social status is not closely allied to income are comparatively few. As income and status are closely reflected in the house one lives in and its locality in general, it follows that occupation and residence are closely related. It has already been seen that residential density varies according to type of suburb, and in New York there is a fairly close correlation between the occupational speciality of a locality and its net density. For example, areas with a speciality in professional occupations have a density of 5·5 per acre; predominantly managerial localities have a density of 4·0; predominantly clerical, 5·31; those with a high proportion of salesmen, 6·5; skilled operatives, 6·77; other operatives, 11·59; and labourers, 21·37. If the pattern of density is a fairly regular one—and in the New York metropolitan region this consists roughly of concentric zones of density—then occupation and social class follow the same zones.

In Liverpool the percentages of occupied men in the five social classes were calculated for the three zones, central, middle, and outer. Classes I and II together (administrative, professional, shopkeepers, and small employers), amounted to 6% in the central zone, 13% in the middle, and 19% in the outer. Class III (clerical service workers, former and skilled workers) also increased outwards, from 39% to 52% to 55%; but semi-skilled and unskilled workers (classes IV and V) decreased from 55% to 35% in the middle zone, and to 26% in the outer zone.

Perhaps the Liverpool example suggests too simple a grading outwards, but, with modification, it can be substantiated in London. Here the centre is more complex, and there is a marked difference between the East End and the West End, the latter having some of the same characteristics as residential midtown Manhattan. Here the percentage in social classes I and II combined may be as high as 34·5% to 46% (Marylebone). In contrast, in the East End the percentage in classes I and II may be as low as 5·5%. There follows a grading outward, but this grading varies considerably. North-eastward it is a slow and gradual one within the conurbation, whereas in the north-west it is sudden, and in places decreases again. In the south the grading is more gradual but eventually gives way to a broad zone where the percentage is again very high. Directly west of London low percentages persist in the manufacturing suburbs. Beyond the conurbation the pattern is broken by centres of trade and industry, but generally speaking the commuting belt has a high proportion in social classes I and II. In a much smaller city like Belfast, local estimates of the social value of certain areas tend to override any concentric pattern, though to the east of the city centre the concentric pattern is seen very well as one moves from the industrial hub, through a more recent lower-middle-class area, to the best residential suburbs on the outskirts.

What is gradually emerging from these examples of density, age differences, occupational and class differences, is that the geographical distribution of each is significant. Moreover the distributions are all interrelated, and it is fairly easy to distinguish localities, each with its own distinctive complex of social characteristics. Whether the total picture in each city, or at least in each Western city, is similar enough to suggest a theory will be discussed below. All that interests us at the moment is that the heterogeneity of a large city does not result in a chaotic and inexplicable confusion, but rather that patterns do emerge which we must try to analyse and explain.

It may well be that the heterogeneity of a pre-industrial city is either more broad, or it may be much finer-grained and appear more homogeneous—as in the extreme examples of West African towns. What is interesting is to see the way in which the indigenous pattern often breaks down and gives way to a modified Western pattern. A good example of this is the residential zoning accepted in 1938 for the city of Damascus. The zones are: 1. artisans—dwellings and workshops; 2. business zone including multi-family dwellings; 3. modern buildings; 4. private homes of (a) shopkeepers and minor civil servants, (b) artisans; 5. private homes of the well-to-do; 6. private homes of the rich—i.e., important civil servants and professional men; 7. private homes of big businessmen, consulates, etc. This zoning is a nice combination of East and West, but it also suggests a fossilizing of a rather over-subdivided structure and one which inclines to diminish mobility.

(v)

Occupation and class are by no means the only ways in which urban society is divided, nor the most rigid. One characteristic of Western cities is the way in which people can and do move from one occupational and status class to another, sometimes very rapidly. Although a section of a city may retain its characteristics as a neighbourhood there may be a considerable turnover in its population; families from a middle-class district often move to an upper-class district and their places are filled by others moving up from the lower status groups. Status or class need not be permanent; it is often recognized by how a person lives, what he does, what he owns, rather than by what he is. It is a very different state of affairs if certain groups are 'foreigners'. Their place in the city is determined by what they are, not by what they do, though the latter often depends on the former. Most large cities are characterized by racial and ethnic heterogeneity. The tendency is to isolate in some way those people who can easily be recognized as being different—either by skin colour or by speaking a different language or by professing different beliefs.

Medieval Caernarfon clearly showed the social divide between the 'foreigners' and the 'natives'. There it was the invading English who created the town and the indigenous Welsh who gathered outside the wall in a suburb; the wall was a cultural divide as well as a defence against attack. On a much larger scale the Tartar city of Peking soon acquired a Chinese city outside its walls. Where cities were indigenous, invaders often formed the appendage. The French fort and sector lay at the southern extremity of Timbuktu; British civil and military lines lay outside Indian cities. The dual nature of the society is always evident in the city plan. When towns were established in Ireland in the 16th and 17th centuries, three 'national' elements were often involved, and even today such towns as Downpatrick and Armagh have their English Street, Scotch Street, and Irish Street radiating from the centre. These were the different quarters, and they were strictly adhered to. The classical instance of the society within a society was the Jewish ghetto, and here the barriers were very rigid indeed. By its very nature the city has attracted diverse peoples, and the diversity is sometimes accentuated, sometimes glossed over, depending on the cultural values both of the original population and of the newcomers.

Divisions in urban society are more likely to be perpetuated if the differences are rooted in race and religion. In such cases the successful working of the city may depend on the acceptance of such differences and the creation of mechanisms to deal with them. The population of Fez has been described as a combination of occupational and ethnic classes together making a mosaic. Only when all the pieces of the mosaic are fitted together is the picture complete. The dominant class in Fez is the Arab Moslem, but within this there are distinctions between the moneyed wholesale class and the retail traders, the artisans and the journeymen. Negro slaves form a distinct group whose tasks are menial. No less segregated are the Jews, who have their own stratification, but who in general link the Moslem population with the outside world, more particularly in finance: a strict Moslem will not deal with banking, and the Jew fulfils this essential economic function. This is a composite society, therefore, in which each group is clearly distinct and exclusive and has a specific job to do. The differences are based on race, religion, and culture.

This kind of rigid caste structure is met in Western cities only where race is the basis of the division. Often the segregation of races arises only when the minority group becomes sufficiently numerous. A sprinkling of another race may be tolerated; a growing concentration provokes reaction, sometimes violent. The word 'segregation' means a sorting-out of two or more groups. If the proportion of Negroes in a city, for example, is evenly distributed so that it is the same in any small part of the city, then segregation does not exist. Normally this is rarely the case. In the major cities of the northeastern United States, Negroes are usually so highly segregated that they form 'black belts' in which they predominate. Perhaps the best-known of these are New York's Harlem and the black belt of Chicago (Fig. 13). Residential mixing is considered so undesirable by other citizens that Negroes find it almost impossible to move from these belts. Densities mount to awful proportions, while restrictive clauses deny the Negroes the right to buy or rent a house in adjoining blocks. These belts began in slum properties, and it is their inability to extend which causes great hardship and mounting tension. The belts tend to be little worlds on their own, almost exclusively coloured and characterized by high densities and low occupational status, which may bring in their train a high incidence of social maladjustments. Under the vigorous segregation policies of some Southern cities of the U.S.A. the pattern of Negro distribution becomes rigid and frozen. A city ordinance of 1919 in Birmingham, Alabama, states: 'It is a misdemeanour for a member of the coloured race to move into, ... or having moved into to continue to reside in, an area of the city of Birmingham generally and historically recognized at the time as an area for occupancy by members of the white race.'

After tremendous pressure the black belt in Chicago has extended southwards from its origin near the city centre into a long narrow strip, about four miles long by half a mile wide. Although the major differences are between the whole belt and the remainder of the city, it also has its own zoning from the point of origin outwards, and these gradations it shares to some extent with the city as a whole. For example the percentage of heads of families born in Southern states drops from 77·7% near the centre to 65·2% at the southern extremity; that of single men decreases from 38·6%

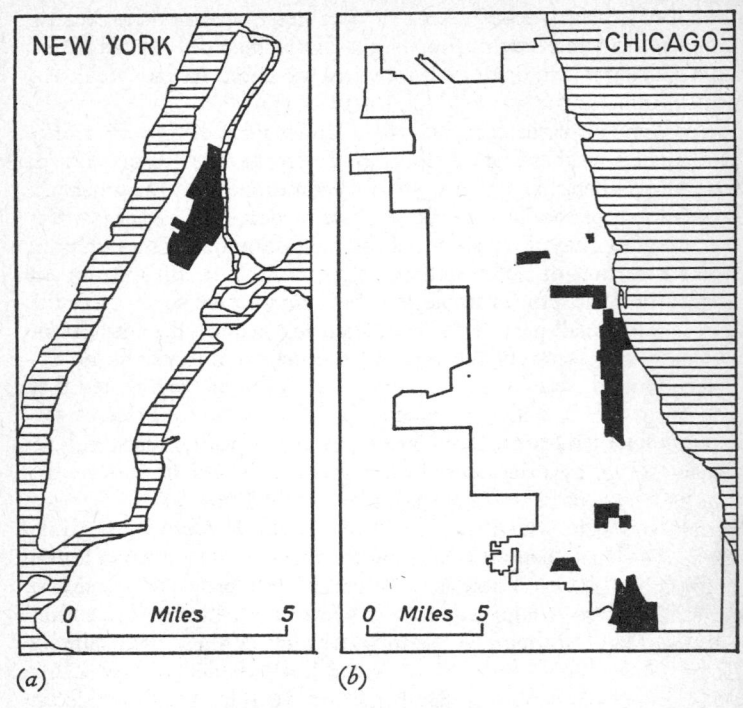

13. Negro segregation: (a) *New York;* (b) *Chicago*

to 24·7%; the percentage of white-collar workers and professional men increases from 5·8% to 34·2%, of skilled workers from 6·2% to 13·0%. Ownership of property increases, juvenile delinquency decreases. This suggests that there is social and actual mobility within the black belt and that the newcomers still tend to come in near the centre of the city and the older-established try to push outwards.

Although it is easy to recognize and map areas in London in which there is a very high incidence of coloured people there is no evidence of a segregated belt. Coloured immigrants are fairly widely scattered around the central area, in general occupying the twilight zones of decaying former middle-class houses as well as smaller terraces of working-class houses. Local concentrations, such as those in Paddington, are hardly segregated compared with American examples. Perhaps the nearest parallel to a belt of coloured people in this country is found in Cardiff, in the so-called Tiger Bay area.

This sector is physically isolated from the remainder of the city, bounded on two sides by docks and river, on a third by the sea, and on the city side by a canal. The physical link is most tenuous. Within this sector, and focused on Loudoun Square, is a population which is about 80% coloured and predominantly Moslem. The nucleus was formed of coloured seamen who were settled there after World War I; seafaring is still high in the occupations. At first coloured men predominated; there were comparatively few women, and they were mostly white. The majority are now of mixed race, but to all intents and purposes this again is a society within a society. The psychological barriers which tend to make this community inward-looking are as strong as the racial reaction which might arise in Cardiff were it to be dispersed in any way.

(vi)

Reaction against peoples of another race is strong, and often violent; and this is why segregation is often rigid. It is less marked among ethnic groups which are 'foreign' to a city. A great deal of research has been done in the United States on the ethnic composition of its cities. Those of the north-east in particular have very high proportions of European migrants, most of whom tend to congregate in distinctive sectors in each city. When Burgess analysed the social composition of Chicago in the 1920s he recognized a 'Deutschland' and a 'Little Sicily'. Most of the industrial cities have their Italian and Polish quarters. In varying degrees they are very distinctive cultural worlds.

The Puerto Ricans in New York are a recent phenomenon. It was not until after the war that they arrived in great numbers, when the granting to them of United States citizenship lowered official barriers. By 1957 there were over half a million in the city. They are by no means as highly segregated as the Negroes, but the majority of them live in 5% of the census tracts of New York, in three fairly well defined areas. Like all new migrants the Puerto Ricans are a young group in which only 13% are over 45 years of age. Predominantly semi-skilled and poorly educated, they are prepared to put up with slum conditions in order to live in New York. They are found, then, in dilapidated and old property which is becoming even more undesirable because of overcrowding. So far they have shown little inclination to move to better areas.

Even more distinctive, because they are more concentrated, are the Italians who live in many up-state New York towns. In Utica, for example, about one person in five is Italian or has one or two

Italian parents. Their distribution in the city is a striking one. They are densely concentrated south of the river and railroad and east of the business district. This sector is characterized by a concentration of industry and commerce, old and poor multi-family houses, cheap rents, and a very high density of population. Only gradually are some Italians moving southward to more pleasant suburbs. To the west of the business district lies a Polish sector, not as accentuated, but quite distinctive, with its own churches, language, and social groups.

All these distributions have something in common. They are in older parts of the cities where property is decayed, where it is possible to live cheaply—even though this is achieved by gross overcrowding. Much of it is slum or near-slum property. The migrant who comes to a city, usually from a poverty-stricken or peasant background, has no choice but to live in those sectors which have been left to decay by their first inhabitants. Later immigrants will add to the concentration, for nothing is more natural than that an Italian coming to Boston or Utica will wish to live near other Italians. In this first generation poverty is usual, education poor, status as low as it can be.

But there are other migrant groups in these cities who do not share these squalid conditions. In Chicago, 'Deutschland' lay beyond the twilight zone, in what Burgess called the zone of working men's homes. In Utica, the Germans live farther from the centre of the city than the Poles, in the suburban western districts, and the Welsh live in the suburban areas beyond the Italian east. The neighbourhoods where German and Welsh are dominant in Utica are middle-class in character. With mixed double- and single-family houses, no industry, and light density, they are generally of quite high status. Why is this difference so marked? One simple reason is that the German and the Welsh are 'old' migrants, who have settled in the city since its inception at the beginning of the last century. The Italians and Poles are 'new', having settled mainly in the 20th century. Moreover the Germans and Welsh came from stock closely allied to the parent Anglo-Saxon stock, and they are Protestant. Italians and Poles are ethnically more different and they are Roman Catholics. In other words the longer acquaintance with Welsh and German and the greater ease of assimilation have meant that they have become more acceptable. They have moved up the social ladder and improved their status; and naturally they have also been able to buy better houses. There is clear evidence in Utica that this happened in the Welsh community. Before this century the Welsh were firmly entrenched in West Utica near the river and the Erie Canal—which they had helped to build. Here three Welsh churches symbolized a distinctive culture group. By 1910 or so this area was 'threatened' by the latest migrant group—the Poles. The Welsh left their ageing houses and moved almost *en bloc* to what was then the newest suburb. Here they rebuilt their churches. They left the canal zone to the Poles.

This introduces an important point concerning ethnic groups. Whereas movement is very difficult for racial groups, to a varying degree, depending on their acceptability in the parent society, ethnic groups are mobile. With progressive assimilation European groups increase their status, and this affects their distribution in the city. More particularly they are able to get away from the zone of slums near the city centre. All the evidence seems to show that migrant groups in the cities of the United States are now less centralized than they were. There is a continual outward movement of migrants. It is also true that the distinction between 'old' and 'new' migrants affects this, the old being much more mobile. This is also closely tied up with their occupations, which in themselves reflect their status on entry; and the length of their residence, which might have enabled them to better themselves. For example, the percentage of labourers among the native whites (Americans) is 4·9%. Among migrants from Germany and England and Wales it is actually lower, but among Poles it is 11·1% and among Italians 15·4%. The proportion of professional and technical workers among the native white is 10·6%, but among the Poles it is as low as 3·7% and among the Italians 2·3%.

Evidence from pre-industrial cities shows some parallels where there are large migrant groups. In Rangoon for example about 30% of the population is composed of Indians and Chinese, and these are considerably segregated from the Burmese. They predominate in the centre, leaving the peripheral areas to the Burmese.

From what has already been said it is clear not only that the areas of cities occupied by migrant ethnic groups are physically distinctive and form a generally recognized pattern, but that the migrant society may also be peculiarly structured. Occupationally and economically they are usually very different from the 'host' society. Even in demographic structure they may be very different, particularly if they are relatively new. Most migrant groups are young and predominantly male. Nearly 14% of the population of Calcutta are excess males, mainly between the ages of 15 and 54. These are migrant workers. Of 140,000 Italians who emigrated in

1950, 66% were men, and 53% of these were between the ages of 20 and 30; only 6·5% were over 50, and 22% of the total were men of between 20 and 30.

The first migrant group in a city, therefore, is very unbalanced. A recent study of Singapore shows not only the difference in age/sex structure among the ethnic groups, but how these change with time. The majority of the population of Singapore are Chinese, but with considerable minorities of Malaysians, Indians, and Pakistanis, together with a small but important minority of Europeans. In 1931 the entire city had an age/sex structure not unlike that of Calcutta, with a heavy preponderance of males, particularly between 20 and 55. Because of their high proportion in the total population this was also the structure of the Chinese group and, in spite of their number, an immigrant feature. The Malaysian society had a much more balanced structure. On the other hand those from India and Pakistan had a structure which was a gross exaggeration of the Chinese, with comparatively few women and children and about 45% in the group of men between 30 and 45. The European age/sex pyramid was typical of the structure in colonies: few women and very few children—particularly of school age—and a preponderance of men over 25 gradually diminishing in the older age groups. By 1957 the structure of the Chinese—and of the total—was well balanced, with a large number of children under 10. The Malaysian pyramid, too, approached the same structure, and even the Indian-Pakistani population was nearer the norm, though still lacking women in the older age groups and having a preponderance of men. The younger men of the administrative class have disappeared in the later European structure and there are more young children; but the dearth of children and adolescents between the ages of 10 and 20 is still very marked. The further back one traces the history of these groups, the more dramatic the changes are seen to be. In 1871 the ratio of Chinese men per 100 women was 630·7; for Indians the male-female ratio was 484·4 per 100, and for Europeans 365·6; the Malaysian ratio was 126·8, not unusual for an indigenous urban population.

(vii)

Race and ethnic differences give rise to the most constant and important differences in urban groups. Another very potent cause for division is religion. Reference has already been made to the ghetto, where segregation was complete. Western cities rarely face segregation based on religion, although, as we shall see, exceptions may be dramatic. In pre-industrial cities divisions may still be sharp. Statistics are rare and difficult to analyse, but one example will give an idea of the heterogeneity which may be found in such a city. The following is a summary of a religious census of Aleppo, a city of 465,966 inhabitants:

Moslems (Sunni)	318,991
Christians	132,799
Jews	14,236

The major differences between these are so great that we can almost disregard the further subdivisions of the Christians into Greek, Armenian, and Syrian Catholics, Greek, Armenian, and Syrian Orthodox, Roman Catholics, Protestants, Maronites, and Chaldeans. It is obvious that ethnic differences cut across doctrinal differences and make divisions even more complex. In most Middle Eastern cities the Shia Moslems would also disclose a fundamental schism in the Islamic world. As far as the three main groups in Aleppo are concerned, the Jews have always lived in the city with the Moslems and have been protected by them because again they were essential to the functioning of the city. But formerly the Christians were entirely segregated outside the walls, and the city gates were closed to them at night. Even today many sections of the city are entirely Moslem, and some are 95% Christian, so that segregation is still high.

A similar situation can arise between Roman Catholics and Protestants in our own cities. The distribution of the Roman Catholic population in Belfast is a striking one. The main concentration forms an axis running from near the city centre in a south-westerly direction along a main routeway into the heart of the country. The point of origin of this axis can be seen on a 17th-century map of Belfast which shows that the walled city built by the English and the Scots had a tiny suburb in the west. There were no Irish (i.e., Roman Catholics) inside the walls, but this cluster of small huts shows that they were being attracted to the new town. It was at exactly this point that their first chapel was built in the late 18th century. In the first half of the 19th century, when industrialization was the great magnet, the Irish flooded into Belfast from the interior and built up this sector along the very route which brought them in. Today it is exclusively Roman Catholic. The segregation is the result of intermittent strife which began when the Protestant majority realized that the Roman Catholic minority was growing (it is now about 1 in 4, but in the mid-19th century it was 1 in 3).

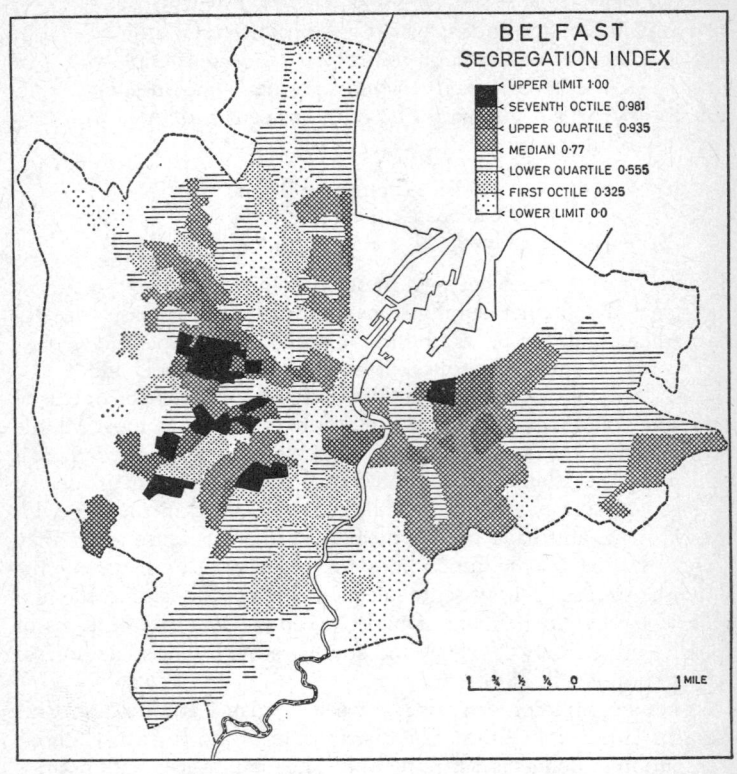

14. Religious segregation (Belfast)

Segregation is measured as the degree to which any district departs from the expected percentage of Roman Catholics if their distribution was random. 25·9%, therefore, indicates no segregation (0·0 as the index), and 0% or 100% is complete segregation (1·00 as the index).

During long intervals of peace and prosperity the edges of the religious districts become blurred, only to sharpen again if rioting breaks out. The accompanying map shows the degree of segregation of these two main sects (Fig. 14). It is assumed that if the percentage of Roman Catholics in any enumeration district is the same as in the city as a whole (25·9), there is no segregation (index: 0·0); if the enumeration district is entirely Roman Catholic or entirely Protestant, segregation is complete (index: 1·00). There are many districts where segregation is absolutely complete. The map, therefore, shows areas of acute separation, and there is a very close correlation between this and occupational status. Segregation is highest in the industrial west and in a zone around the centre where occupational status is low. Segregation lessens in the more residential areas, and is least in the middle-class suburbs.

(viii)
Enough has been said to show that the heterogeneity of a city's people gives rise to complex social patterns. There are towns within towns, cultures within cultures. Societies are split radically by differences such as those of race and creed which can never be overcome. Superimposed on these are the dividing-lines of occupation and class, across which some move readily, others hardly at all. The rigidity or otherwise of each group is reflected either in its inability to move within the city or in its choice of movement. Because of all these elements the city is revealed not as a uniform whole, but as a mass of differentiated, interlocking parts, alive, colourful, dynamic. The total impression is of a confusion of types, of different colours, different creeds, the young, the old, the rich, and the poor. Yet in a sense some of these belong more to one part than to another. In this amazing perplexity of human types there is a sorting-out process. Almost imperceptibly we see that these avenues are the property of the old, these terraces of the young, this block is white and this block black, this is a Protestant neighbourhood, this a Roman Catholic, here are the rich, there the poor. There is obviously a close connexion between locality, between the city environment—type and age of houses for example—and certain social groups. This has been implicit throughout this chapter and more than once the point has been explicitly made.

In Britain there is a straightforward correlation between the desirability of a neighbourhood and class. A pleasant environment, spacious gardens, larger houses of recent construction, parks, absence of industry—all these things must be paid for; and in the past—the past which we have inherited in the cities of today—this was clearly the prerogative of the middle and upper classes. In contrast to these suburbs were the physically repellent areas, unfortunately the greater part of most of our industrial cities, which were clearly the world of the manual workers. This distinction is true today in all the older sections of our Victorian cities: it is rapidly breaking down both in modern extensions and in new towns. The total urban environment is now considered to be of primary importance, and paradoxically, because the planned neighbourhood is the concern of public rather than of private enterprise, the scales may now be tipped slightly in favour of the manual worker, even if his house is still small. But in so far as the vast majority still live in the cities of the last century, the old division still holds good.

Differences based on colour, language, nationality fit into this simplified class pattern. Immigrants to a city almost invariably come in at the lowest point in the class structure. Usually unskilled and with no resources, they first congregate in the poorest part of the city: that is, the oldest, run-down areas from which others are moving after improving their lot. This has been true throughout the history of migrant groups in the cities of north-eastern United States. It is equally true of coloured migrants in London or Leeds. The streets into which they move may be old industrial houses, or former middle-class terraces and squares which the original inhabitants have long ago left to decay; the latter are the houses which become slums, where former spaciousness has been turned into intolerable overcrowding, and dignity has been turned into degradation. This is not to argue that the environment creates the social group or that groups create the environment. It is a much more complex process which arises from two basic facts. The first is that cities age. In a sense the process of decay begins as soon as building is complete; and although some may be artificially preserved, the majority become degraded both in upkeep and amenities. The second fact is that society is dynamic and mobile. Even in the older ethnic areas there is often a constant coming and going. Many ethnic areas are preserved, not because people do not move, but because those that move are replaced by newcomers. So in spite of mobility certain group characteristics can still be very closely tied to easily identified sectors of the city.

If this is so, do such differences suggest any kind of pattern which is uniform for all cities? It is generally assumed that slum areas are found near the centre of most large industrial cities. The word 'slum' is often used loosely to indicate social conditions as well as poor housing. 'Overcrowded' expresses the former and 'unfit to live in' the latter. Both would be very difficult to define, though structural defects and failure to comply with certain minimum sanitary and other standards can now be applied for official slum-clearance purposes. It is these latter criteria which enable us to recognize 'zones of decay' in our larger cities, and these so often surround the business and shopping centres. Ageing begins in the centre and works outwards. The centre of the modern city—

although it may still have small pockets of decay—is usually quite new. Rebuilding to meet the increasing needs of the centre of a growing city means the demolition of the old. Most often the newest buildings of all are found on the rim of the city centre, where the centre itself is expanding into what is now the oldest remaining part of the city; so the newest and the oldest are cheek by jowl. Around this rebuilt centre, then, is a zone which is old—if not entirely decayed—and here housing is bound to be out of phase with the basic requirements of life today. Here there will be a great variety of house types—small industrial houses, often in conjunction with factories and warehouses, or large middle- and upper-class squares. They all have one thing in common, and that is age. There are many reasons why some of the latter may be saved from utter decay—usually by changing their function—but if they continue as residences they almost invariably become crowded with migrants or very poor families for whom lack of amenities is acceptable either because rents are cheaper or because they have no choice. The smaller terraces have a better chance of retaining their dignity and cleanliness, but are often classified as slums because their amenities fall below official standards.

In Belfast, with two small exceptions, such conditions ring the entire city centre (Fig. 15). For a depth of half a mile or so this zone is a mass of small terrace houses all characterized by having no back access, which means they were built before the 1870s. They are interspersed with industrial areas, docks, railway yards, gas works. Two slender lines of larger houses break the circle. They date from the same period. Some have become slums, where overcrowding is infinitely worse than in the small terraces; some have been preserved by becoming doctors' and dentists' surgeries. I have taken Belfast as an example of the accepted pattern of the zone of decay because there is evidence of what the conditions were in the city over a century ago (Fig. 16). In the 1820s there was a fairly clear distinction between a residential area to the south of the centre, the beginnings of an industrial western sector, and the dockland area to the north. The overcrowded and insanitary areas were found in small pockets in the centre of the town itself, and in the west and north. The first disappeared with rebuilding, but by the 1850s the other two had expanded with the growth of the town and were beginning to close the ring to the north of the city centre; while to the south and near the river a new slum area had appeared near the gas works. The southern sector of industrial terraced houses had not then been built, but already much of the later pattern is

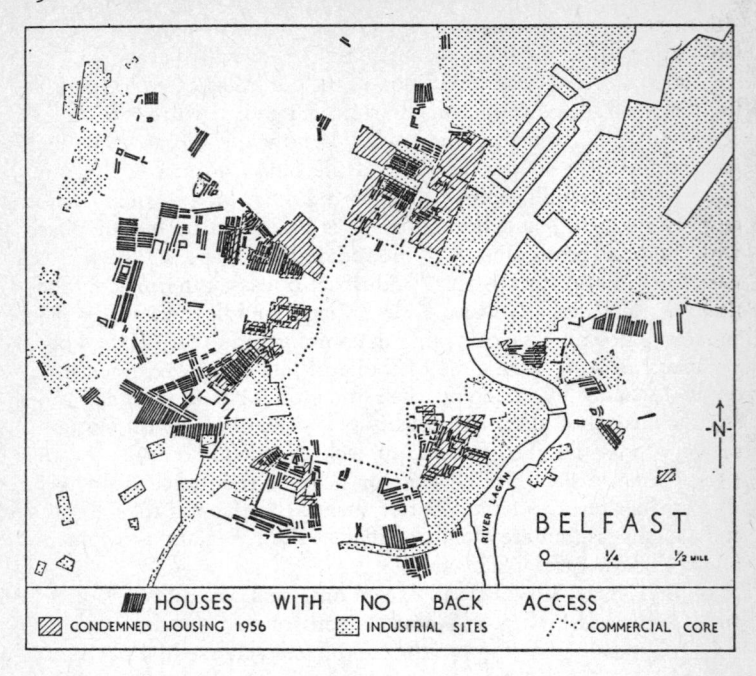

15. Zone of old and condemned houses (Belfast)

evident. What is even more interesting is the impression that the slum areas had growth points from which they expanded, suggesting that age and decay alone are not a sufficient explanation. Certainly the earlier slums bore a similar relationship to the old town as the decayed areas of today bear to the modern city.

Is this progression from the rebuilt centre, through a zone of decay, to the newer residential areas universally applicable? Not necessarily in Western cities and certainly not in the pre-industrial city. Our preconceived ideas of approaching a city through pleasant suburbs would receive a severe shock in Asia or Latin America. One of the unmistakable impressions on arriving in a Latin American city is having to drive through the slum areas on the outskirts. The pattern seems to have been reversed. I have already referred to the nature of these shanty towns. What we are now interested in is their distribution, and the fact—referred to earlier—that they are not slums in the conventional Western sense of the word. As I

BELFAST ZONES OF DECAY

OVERCROWDED AREAS 1824
SLUM AREAS 1840-1852
SLUM AREAS, M.O.H. 1852
CONDEMNED HOUSES 1956
MODERN LIMIT OF NON RESIDENTIAL CITY CENTRE

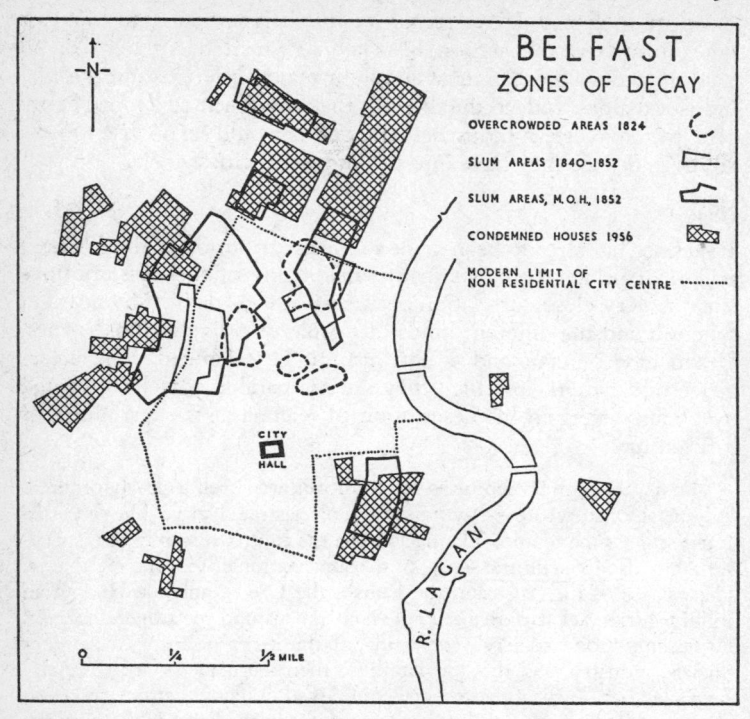

16. *The growth of slum areas (Belfast)*

said previously, far from being areas of decay, they are growth points. This is not a justification of their continuance or of their gross inadequacies, but a recognition of the attitude of the people who live in them and the fact that they are often capable, on rebuilding, of becoming an intrinsic and acceptable part of the fabric of the city. Whereas our suburbs push urban values into the countryside, the shanty town has brought rural values into the city. Their assimilation depends on how temporary such additions are viewed to be, and with what degree of tolerance.

These two areas of change in cities, the Western slum and its decay, and the pre-industrial shanty town with its possibilities of achieving urban acceptance, have been highlighted to suggest that a pattern may exist which arises from the fact that cities are rarely static, and even if they are not growing, time is inexorably at work in creating change. If we recognize this it is tempting to look for generalizations and suggest lines along which the pattern of all cities may develop. We must allow for major differences in the pre-industrial cities. Indeed the theories that have been developed apply only to the Western industrial city, and it would be unwise to read any significance they have into pre-industrial cities.

(ix)

Reference has already been made to the contribution of the Chicago school of urban ecologists in this field. One of their assumptions was the very close correlation between zones as defined by age and function and the different kinds of people who live in those zones. Urban environment and society cannot be separated. The emergence of a pattern in which they are inseparable is well illustrated by Stefan Zweig in his description of Vienna at the beginning of this century:

> Vienna, through its centuries-old tradition, was itself a clearly ordered, and—as I once wrote—a wonderfully orchestrated city. The Imperial house still set the tempo. The palace was the centre, not only in a spatial sense but also in a cultural sense, of the supernationality of the monarchy. The palaces of the Austrian, the Polish, the Czech, and the Hungarian nobility formed as it were a second enclosure around the Imperial palace. Then came 'good society', consisting of the lesser nobility, the higher officials, industry, and the 'old families', then the petty bourgeoisie and the proletariat. Each of these social strata lived in its own circle, and even in its own district, the nobility in their palaces in the heart of the city, the diplomats in the third district, industry and the merchants in the vicinity of the Ringstrasse, the petty bourgeoisie in the inner districts—the second to the ninth—and the proletariat in the outer circle. But everyone met in the theatre and at the great festivities such as the Flower Parade in the Prater, where three hundred thousand people enthusiastically applauded the 'upper ten thousand' in their beautifully decorated carriages.[1]

This is strangely reminiscent of the pattern of society which may have been characteristic of Mayan cities. It is certainly a picture of the renaissance city and is nearer the pre-industrial than the industrial city. Its interest to us now is the concentric zoning rather than the sequence of zones. The first theory concerning the social pattern of the Western city, put forward by E. W. Burgess was in fact one of concentric zones (Fig. 17). According to Burgess, as a result of expansion from the centre and subsequent ageing, there are five concentric zones in Chicago:

[1] S. Zweig, *The World of Yesterday*, Cassell & Co., London, 1942.

(i) A central business district; this is the skyscraper zone which has been rebuilt and replaced the oldest part of the city.
(ii) Around the central business district is a zone of old buildings including tenements, rooming areas, scattered business premises and light industries. This he calls the zone of transition.
(iii) Next comes a zone of single- and two-family dwellings, followed by:
(iv) An exclusively residential suburban zone. Finally this merges into:
(v) A commuting zone.

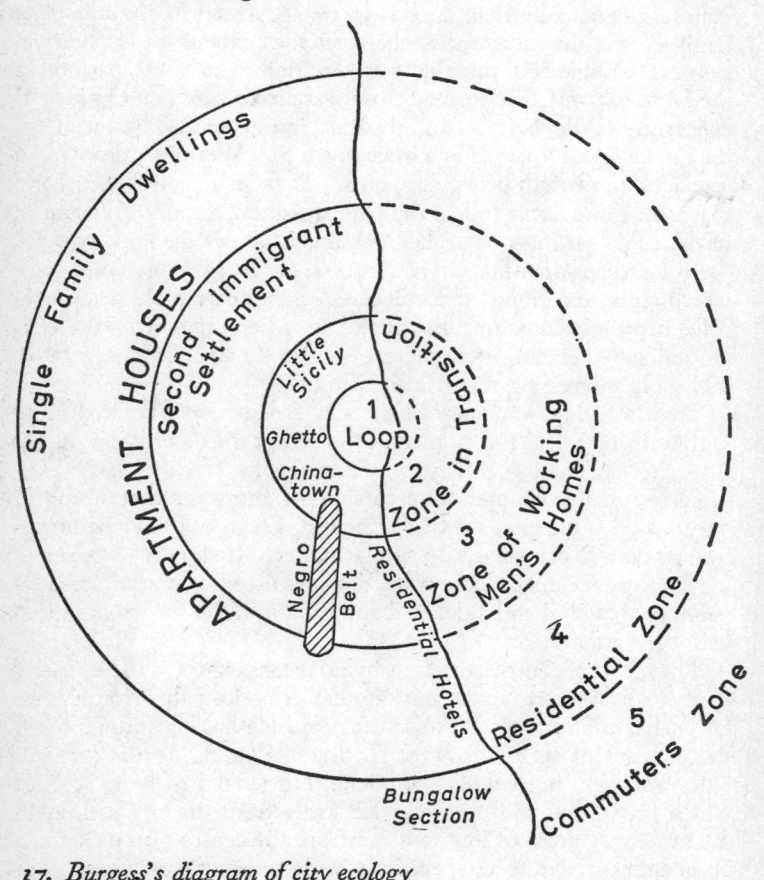

17. *Burgess's diagram of city ecology*

Each of these zones tends to expand at the expense of the one on its outer edge, giving continual change. Coupled with these age and function zones are the activities of different groups of people. The innermost area has little permanent population, but sees a vast daily movement in and out. The zone of transition houses those groups which have recently arrived in America—immigrants which make up a ghetto or a 'Little Sicily'—the Negro population, which finds movement almost impossible, and those who have no roots in any society, transients and lawbreakers. The third zone is the working-class district, and here too are found second-generation immigrants who have freed themselves socially from the inner zone. The residential suburban zone is of stable 'American' middle-class families, and the same social characteristics extend into zone five. Burgess emphasized that he was describing an ideal pattern, a model to which Chicago very closely approximated; and he would expect to find deviations from the ideal in most cities. Nevertheless the model is put forward as a basic one for all Western cities. Given the fact that growth takes place outwards from a central point, and that ageing and decay follow the same direction, a concentric pattern results. The sorting-out of the population follows the same pattern. 'In the expansion of a city a process of distribution takes place which sifts and sorts and relocates individuals and groups by residence or occupation. The resulting differentiation of the cosmopolitan American city into areas is typically all from one pattern, with only interesting minor modifications.'

This is a deterministic-mechanistic explanation of social areas within the city. For the moment let us accept the description, rather than the explanation. Many of the social facts which have been discussed in this chapter seem to support Burgess's description in very broad outline. Data from London, Liverpool, and Belfast as well as New York suggest a similar pattern. It should be borne in mind, however, that much of the data discussed were abstracted by zones of this kind and a detailed application of the theory has in no way been attempted.

The ideal concentric pattern is by no means expected to be strictly true of all Western cities, but another American theorist, Homer Hoyt, has found it totally unsatisfactory. He has substituted for it the concept of sector growth. He found that residential areas of high rent were not simply peripheral, but tended to be in wedges which broadened as they expanded away from the city centre. In the same way areas of low rent ran from the centre of the city in a broadening wedge to the periphery without substantially changing character. Hoyt assumes that these differences are initiated at a very early stage in the city's history, and once a point has a certain residential character, this character is maintained in the outward growth of that point. Expansion can only be outwards because other growth points having a different character will also be growing and will prevent lateral expansion of the first characteristic. The result is a series of sectors which run from near the centre to the periphery of the city. Again the sorting-out process of human groups which follow the same pattern is mechanistic.

Earlier in this chapter it was suggested that the slum areas of Belfast can be shown to have moved in a way which would fit in with Hoyt's theory. Even more striking in Belfast is the way in which the high-class residential area in the south has grown into a sector almost exactly as Hoyt described in an ideal situation. This sector originated on the southern edge of the embryonic city of Belfast and in the 18th and 19th century it expanded steadily southward; to the east industrialization and the river Lagan prevented lateral expansion, and to the west an industrial sector, which had its origins to the west of the early city, similarly prevented a lateral spread. The wedge-shape of residential South Belfast is still preserved.

It is quite obvious that the answer to our search for an ideal pattern is no simple one. Attractive though Burgess's and Hoyt's schemes are, they are mutually exclusive. Although they have made a great contribution to urban studies they are both relatively unsophisticated and only acceptable to those who are also prepared to accept the deterministic sorting-out of society which is implied in each. Their lack of sophistication may well have arisen from the fact that they were based on American cities, most of which are of recent growth and uncomplicated by historical inertia. It is significant that the American protest to both theories came from Boston. Here, Walter Firey found that he was dealing with a unique pattern which could be explained only in non-rational terms like 'social value'. The reason why Beacon Hill in Boston had retained its historic residential character—and defied any 'normal' process of city growth—was an irrational one which arose from the social value given to the area by those who lived there.

One is constantly aware of such irrational factors in our own cities. Examining the previous example of South Belfast's residential area in more detail we find that the area now covered by the outer part of the wedge had a very distinctive character long before the city started expanding. It was a rich parkland situated on a ridge of sands and gravels which, moreover, carried the all-important road to

Dublin. It was an 'upper-class' area long before the city crept towards it. In the same way the western area was thoroughly industrialized *before* it was absorbed by the expanding western sector. In other words the city did not expand into socially 'neutral' country, but into areas which already had very distinctive social values; and these, as much as anything else, set the tone of the residential areas which eventually spread over them.

Does this mean that each city is unique and that we are wasting our time in looking for generalization? Only to a certain degree. In so far as certain trends have been allowed to fashion our cities, these must be discovered and analysed, but it must be realized that the trends are the sum total of human action and decision, and these need not always conform to an idealized pattern. 'Irrationality'—so called merely because it disturbs too simple a pattern and too simple an explanation—must be written into any theory on city organization and growth. More important than this even is the fact that the theory must be related to a wider cultural context: other cultures, both in space and time, will set a different framework within which to look for generalized patterns.

This book began with a discussion of the many approaches which have been made to the study of the city, from the viewpoint of history, of function, of regional relationships, of planning, and of society. The final paragraphs suggest two things: (a) that generalizations—however narrow or naïve or unsophisticated, and however much at variance with the uniqueness of cities—must still be looked for, and chaos resolved into intelligible patterns; (b) that ultimately it is with man's behaviour we are dealing, and that it is society that makes the pattern we are trying to discover.

Bibliography

(in addition to articles referred to in footnotes)

General

Beaujeu-Garnier, J., and Chabot, G., *Traité de géographie urbaine*, Paris, 1963.
Elias, C. E., Gillies, J., and Reimer, S., *Metropolis: Values in Conflict*, Belmont, Calif., 1964.
George, P., *La Ville*, Paris, 1952.
Houston, J. M., *A Social Geography of Europe*, London, 1953.
Rasmussen, S., *London the Unique City*, New York, 1951.
Reissman, L., *The Urban Process*, London, 1964.
Robson, W. A., *Great Cities of the World*, London, 1957.
Smailes, A. E., *The Geography of Towns*, London, 1960.

Chapter 1

Briggs, A., *Victorian Cities*, London, 1963.
Geddes, P., *Cities in Evolution*, London, 1915.
Harris, C. D., and Ullman, E. L., 'The Nature of Cities', *Annals of the American Academy of Political and Social Science*, 1945.
Jones, E., *The City in Geography*, London, 1963.
Mumford, L., *The City in History*, London, 1961.
Park, R. E., Burgess, E. W., and McKenzie, R. D., *The City*, Chicago, 1925.
Weber, M., *The City* (English translation), London, 1960.

Chapter 2

Bulsara, J. F., *Problems of Rapid Urbanisation in India*, Bombay, 1964.
Green, C. M., *American Cities in the Growth of the Nation*, London, 1954.
Hauser, P. (ed.), *Urbanisation in Latin America*, Paris, 1961.
Jones, E., 'Aspects of Urbanisation in Venezuela', *Ekistics*, XVIII, 109, 1964.
Morley, S. G., *The Maya Civilisation*, Los Angeles, 1954.
Piggott, S., *Prehistoric India*, London, 1950.
Pirenne, H., *Medieval Cities*, Princeton, 1925.
Turner, R. (ed.), *India's Urban Future*, California, 1962.
Wycherley, R. E., *How the Greeks Built Cities*, London, 1949.
United Nations, *Demographic Year Book*, New York, 1960.

United Nations, *Report on the World Social Situation*, New York, 1957.
'Urbanism in West Africa', *Sociological Review*, VII, 1, 1959.

Chapter 3

Berger, M. (ed.), *The New Metropolis in the Arab World*, London, 1963.
Caplow, T., 'The Social Ecology of Guatemala', *Social Forces*, XXVIII, 1949.
Hayner, N. S., 'Mexico City', *American Journal of Sociology*, LI, 1945.
Miner, H., *The Primitive City of Timbuctoo*, Princeton, 1953.
Sjoberg, G., *The Pre-Industrial City*, Glencoe, Ill., 1960.
Trewartha, G., 'Chinese Cities', *Annals of the Association of American Geographers*, XLII, 1952.

Chapter 4

Dickinson, R. E., *The West European City*, London, 1951.
Freeman, T. W., *The Conurbations of Great Britain*, Manchester, 1959.
Gallion, A. B., and Eisner, S., *The Urban Pattern*, New York, 1963.
Gottmann, J., *Megalopolis*, London, 1963.
Howard, E., *Garden Cities of Tomorrow*, London, 1902.
Lynch, K., 'The Pattern of the Metropolis' in *The Future Metropolis* (ed. Ll. Rodwin), London, 1962.
Murphy, R. E., and Vance, J. E., 'Delimiting the C.B.D.', *Economic Geography*, XXX, 1954.
Queen, S. A., and Carpenter, D. B., *The American City*, London, 1953.
Self, P., *Cities in Flood*, London, 1957.

Chapter 5

Carruthers, I., 'A Classification of Service Centres in England and Wales', *Geographical Journal*, CXXIII, 1957.
Christaller, W., *Die Zentralen Orte Suddeutschlands*, Jena, 1933.
Moser, C. A., and Scott, W., *British Towns*, London, 1961.
Zipf, G. K., *National Unity and Disunity*, Bloomington, Ind., 1941.

Chapter 6

Bracey, H. E., 'Towns as Rural Service Centres', *Transactions of the Institute of British Geographers*, 1953.
Dickinson, R. E., *City and Region*, London, 1964.
Duncan, O. D., et al., *Metropolis and Region*, Baltimore, 1960.
Fawcett, C. B., *The Provinces of England*, London, 1919.
Gilbert, E. W., 'Practical Regionalism in England and Wales', *Geographical Journal*, XCIV, 1939.

Chapter 7

Burgess, E. W., and Bogue, D. J., *Contributions to Urban Sociology*, Chicago, 1964.
Centre for Urban Studies, *London: Aspects of Change*, London, 1964.
Firey, W., *Land Use in Central Boston*, Cambridge, Mass., 1947.
Gittus, E., 'Social Structure' in *A Scientific Survey of Merseyside* (ed. W. Smith), Liverpool, 1953.

Hawley, A., *Human Ecology*, New York, 1950.
Hoyt, H., *The Structure and Growth of Residential Neighbourhoods in American Cities*, Washington, 1939.
Jones, E., *A Social Geography of Belfast*, London, 1961.
Lieberson, S., *Ethnic Patterns in American Cities*, Glencoe, Ill., 1963.
Liepmann, K., *The Journey to Work*, London, 1944.
Neville, R. J. W., 'Singapore; Recent Trends in Sex and Age Composition of a Cosmopolitan Community', *Population Studies*, XVII, 1963.
Reiss, A. J., and Hatt, P. K., *Cities and Society*, Glencoe, Ill., 1957.
Theodorson, G. A. (ed.), *Studies in Human Ecology*, New York, 1961.

Index

Abercrombie, Sir Patrick, 65–67, 102
Aberystwyth, 89, 100
administrative areas, 74, 95–96; functions of towns, 3, 4
Africa: sex ratio, 115; towns and cities, 34–35, 39; urbanization, 14, 16, 34–35
age groups, distribution of, 116–21, 130; sex differences, 118–20
agricultural communities (*see also* peasant communities), 17, 39, 40
agriculture, 3, 4, 105; innovations, 25; productivity, 29, 66
Aleppo, religious census, 131
Algeria, 4, 14
Amsterdam, 27, 72
Ankara, 83, 84
Antwerp, 27
Argentina: fertility ratio, 116; infantile mortality, 116; size of cities, 37, 81–82; *villas de miseria*, 50
Asia: age groups, 117; fertility ratio, 116; outskirts of cities, 50, 136; sex ratio, 114–15; towns and cities, 35–36, 39, 46, 48; urbanization, 2, 14, 16, 34–36
Athens, 6, 23
Australia, 13, 29
Austria, 82, 84
avenues, 28, 49, 54–55
Aztecs, 23, 36, 48

Babylon, 21–22
Baghdad, 77
Bahrein, 14, 16, 35
Barbican, London, 70
bastide towns, 26, 45, 49
Bath, 28, 53, 54
Belfast: age groups, 117–20, (*map*) 118; density, 105–7; influence, 100–1; population growth, 55; religious segregation, 131–3, (*map*) 132; residential areas, 56, 122–3, 141–2; slums, 135–6, 141, (*maps*) 136–7; social areas, 122–3, 140; water supply, 94–95
Berlin, 28, 32
Birmingham, Alabama, 125
Birmingham, England: influence, 100, 101; manufacturing centre, 77, 89; office space, 75, 110; population, 84; water supply, 95
Bogota, 48
Bombay, 36, 113, 116
Boston, 69, 108, 117, 128, 141
boundaries, 33, 96
Brasilia, 84
Brazil, 16, 37, 50
Briggs, A., 6, 58
Bristol, 27, 80, 100, 105
Britain (*see also* Scotland *and* Wales): age grouping, 117; classification of towns, 90, 92; definition of towns and cities, 4; density of cities, 105, 108; fertility ratio, 116; industrial revolution, 29–30; infantile mortality, 115–16; market towns, 93–94; population changes, 25; Roman towns, 24–25; sex ratio, 114; size of towns and cities, 82–84, (*table*) 84; towns and cities, 27–30, 52, 56, 58, (*plan*) 57; urban population, 2, 13, 30; urbanization, 13–14, 16–17
Bruges, 27
Buenos Aires, 37, 48, 49, 116
buildings, monumental, 20, 22–23, 28, 49, 54, 58–59
Bulgaria, 16, 30, 31
Burgess, E. W., 9, 127–8, 138–41

INDEX

buses, 60; frequencies, 99, 100; local service regions (*map*) 98
business district, central (*see also* offices), 43, 49, 74, 75, 108, 139
by-laws governing building of houses, Victorian: *see under* houses and housing

Caernarfon, 26, 45–46, 53, 124
Calcutta: age groups, 117; densities, 43, 105, 113; homeless, 44, 51; migrant workers, 129–30; population, 32, 36
Canada, 3, 16
canals as streets, 44, 48
Canberra, 83
capital cities, 27–28, 54–55, 81–84, 86, 94, (*table*) 82
Caracas, 37, 50–51, (*map*) 47
Cardiff, 80, 126–7
castles, 25, 53–54
catchment areas, 97, 99
cathedrals, 48, 49, 53
census, 3, 33, 64, 91, 106–8, 121
Central America, 14, 18
central place theory, 85
centre of towns and cities, 22, 49, 61–63, 68, 70–74, 77, 108–13; age-group structure, 119–21; densities, 107–8, 112–13; markets, 40–42, 46, 62; movement away from, 32–33, 111–12; rebuilding, 134–6; shopping, 38, 41, 43, 49, 62
chequerboard town, 26
Chester, 24, 26, 53
Chicago, black belt, 125–6, (*map*) 126; centre, 61, 75; concentric zones, 138–40; density, 108–9; ecological school, 9, 138; Loop area, 62, 109; population, 32; social composition, 127–8; street pattern, 59, (*map*) 57
Chichen Itza, 22
Childe, V. G., 17–20, 23
children, number of, 116–21, 130
Chile, 16, 37, 50, 81–82
China, 18, 36, 39, 44–47, 84, 115
Christaller, W., 85–86, 93, 97
Chungking, 44–45, (*map*) 41
Church, role of the, 24, 26, 45
church, 26, 45, 49, 53, 59
'citadel', 21

cities: differences from towns (*see also* definitions), 4–5; common elements, 38–40, 46, 47, 52; forms (*illus.*), 70
'city regions', 97, 101–2
civitas, 96
class structure, 40, 67, 104, 134; age pattern, 120; and housing, 40, 43–44, 52, 122–3; movement from one status to another, 123–4; occupation and, 40, 121–4
classification of towns and cities, 80–92
coal-mining, 29, 55, 89
Colombia, 16, 48
coloured people (*see also* Negroes), 126–7
commercial function of cities, 6–7, 10, 25, 27
communications, 8–10, 25, 33, 72–73
commuting and commuters, 60, 62, 66, 68, 102, 108–11, 113, 139
concentric zoning, 9, 138–40
Congo, 4
conurbations, 12, 33, 64, 69–70, 102, 109
Conway, 45, 114
Cooley, C. H., 10
Copal, 22
Copenhagen, 28, 71, 116
core city, 70–71
Cornwall, bus services, (*map*) 98
counties, 96
countryside, contrasts between town and, 10, 115; economic dependence of towns on, 10, 93; English people and, 2; habits and traditions, 105; links with towns, 93, 95, 97, 99, 103; occupations, 121; sex ratio, 114, 115; urban ideas in, 78–79
county boroughs, 96
crossroads symbol, 7–10
Czechoslovakia, 4

Damascus, 123
Dar-es-Salaam, 35
decay, areas of, 134–7
decentralization of population and industry, 64–65
decline of cities, 12

defence, 7, 12, 28, 40, 44, 46, 124
definitions of towns and cities, 3–5, 7, 14, 38
Delhi, 43, 105, 113
Denmark, 3, 16, 84, 116
densities, of towns and cities, 3–5, 8, 43, 66–67, 72–73, 91–92, 104–9, 112–13, 122; housing, 43, 66, 70–71, 106–8, 122–3
Dickinson, R. E., 10
dispersed cities, 70, 72–73, 105
distribution of towns, 85–89
Dominican Republic, 4

ecclesiastical districts, 96
ecology, 9, 11, 138–9
economic factors in urbanization, 6–7, 10–11, 17, 96; economic dependence on countryside, 10, 93; economic dominance of city, 101
Edinburgh: centre, 53–54, 73–74, (map) 53; density, 105; tall buildings, 26, 45
education (see also schools), 86, 89, 90
Egypt, 10, 18, 20, 23
environments, 9–10, 94–95, 104, 133–4, 138
ethnic groups, 42, 124, 127–30, 134
Europe, central 82; eastern, 81; medieval, 6; sex ratio, 114; towns and cities, 12, 38–39; 45, 49, 52–79, 96; urbanization, 2, 14, 16–17, 23–33, 39
evolutionary stages of cities, 12

factories and mills, 56, 61
fairs, 25
families, ties, 8; size, 105, 116
farming and farmers, 88, 93–94, 105
fertility ratio, 116
Fez, 124
Finland, 3
Firey, Walter, 141
food, distribution, 99; producing, 10, 12, 17–19, 22, 25, 72
'foreigners' in cities, 124, 127
France: *bastide* towns, 45; city regions, 86–87, (map) 87; industrial revolution, 29; infantile mortality, 116; size of cities, 81–82; urban population, 30–31

functions of towns and cities, 4–5, 11, 88–91

garden cities, 65–66, 73
Geddes, P., 12, 33
geographers, and study of cities, 9–11, 97
Germany: industrial revolution, 29; medieval towns, 27; southern, 86; urban population, 30–31
Ghana, 3, 14
Gottmann, J., 33, 69
Greater London Authority, 102
Greece: Greek cities, 20, 23, 46, 49, 59; city states, 6, 10, 23, 93, 96; definition of town, 3
Green, F. H. W., 99, 100
green belts, 64–65, 69, 102, 107, 110, 112
grid road system, 20–21, 24, 28, 31–32 48–49, 54–55, 59, 73
guilds, 26, 45
Guinea, 14

Harappa, 20–21, 46
Harlem, 125
Harris, C. D., 90, 91
Haussmann, Baron, 55
Health Act (1875), 56
Hemel Hempstead, 69, (map) 68
heterogeneity, social, 8, 40, 42, 105–6, 123–4, 131, 133
hexagonal hierarchy of regions, 85–87, 93, 97, (illus.) 86
'hinterland', 97
historical study of cities, 5, 6
hospitals, 26, 89, 100
houses and housing, 40, 51; by-laws governing building standards (Victorian, 21, 30, 52, 56, 106, 119; class and, 40, 43–44, 52, 122–3; densities, 43, 66, 70–71, 106–8, 122–3; estates, 65; migrant groups, 134–5; moving house, 111, 123; poor, 43, 134–7, 141; styles of houses, 60–61, 67
Housing Repairs and Rent Act (1954), 56
Howard, E., 65–67
Hoyt, H., 140–1
Hungary, 16

INDEX

Ife, 35
Incas, 23, 36, 48
India: British in, 124; cities, 35, 39, 42–44; definition of town, 3–4; farmers, 105; fertility ratio, 116; size of cities, 84; urbanization, 14, 16, 35
Indonesia, 14
Indus Valley, 18–20
industrial estates, 61, 65; revolution, 18, 28–31, 38–39, 55, 59–60, 77; towns, 29–31, 38–39, 55–56, 59, 61, 127, (*illus.*) 57
industrialization, 17, 31, 34–37, 39, 47
infantile mortality, 115–16
influence of towns, regions of, 97–103, (*illus.*) 98
Iraq, 14, 46
Israel, 4, 14, 16, 35
Italy, 20, 82, 83

Japan, 4, 14, 35, 114–16
Jefferson, Mark, 54, 81, 83
Jews, 77, 124; ghetto, 124, 130, 140
Johannesburg, 35
Jordan, 14

Kenya, 14
Kinshasa (Léopoldville), 35
Korea, 84
Kunming, 115

land use, 52, 61–62, 76, 78, 107
Landa, 22
La Paz, 48
Latin America: age groups, 117; fertility ratio, 116; infantile mortality, 116; sex ratio, 114–15; shanty towns, 37, 50–51, 136; slum areas, 136; Spanish and Portuguese in, 36, 48; towns and cities, 34, 36–37, 39, 47–50, 51; urbanization, 2, 14, 16–17, 34, 36–37, 47–50
Leeds, 29, 58, 100, 134
L'Enfant, Pierre, 54–55
Letchworth, 65–66
Lima, 37, 50
linear town, 70, 71
Lisbon, 27
Liverpool: age groups, 120; cellars as dwellings, 56; concentric pattern, 140; conurbation, 107; density, 107, 122; population, 84, 112; regional relationships, 100; water supply, 95
local authorities, 96
London: administration, 102; age groups, 120–1; areas of specialized functions, 76–78, (*map*) 76; classification, 91; coloured immigrants, 126, 134; commuting, 109–10; concentric pattern, 140; conurbation, 64, 70; County, 75, 102, 109–10; County of London Plan (1943), 67; densities, 107–9; fertility ratio, 116; Greater London Plan (1944), 65; green belt, 64–65, 102, 107, 110, 112; growth, 2, 64, 65; housing, 112; infantile mortality, 116; medieval street pattern, 54; occupations and residential density, 122; offices, 2, 75, 110; population changes, 27–28, 32–33, 111–12; regions of influence, 88, 101–2, (*map*) 98; reshaping plan, 71; services, 11; size 80, 84; study of, 6; traffic, 62; water supply, 95
London County Council, 65, 107, 112
Lopez, R. S., 7–8
Los Angeles, 63, 73, 95

McKenzie, R. D., 9
Madrid, 81, 82
Maine, H. S., 7
Maitland, F. W., 7
Manchester: growth, 64; influence, 100, 101; offices, 75, 110; population, 55, 84
Mandalay, 39, 46
manufacturing, 7, 26, 29, 40, 55, 77–78, 84, 90–91, 105
market place, 23, 26, 45, 53; towns, 6, 11, 25, 80–81, 89, 93–94, 96, 100; regions of influence, 93–94, 99, (*illus.*) 98
marketing function, 11, 25, 88–89
markets, 3, 6, 26, 40–42, 46, 62, 93–94
Mata, Sorina y, 71

INDEX

Mayans, 18, 20, 22, 36, 48, 138
medieval towns and cities, 4, 6, 25–27, 39, 45, 52–54, 58–59, 94
megalopolis, 2, 12, 33, 69, 101
Mesopotamia, 18, 21, 23
metropolitan cities, 33, 101
Mexico, 37, 48, 116
Mexico City, 48, 49, 116
Middle East, 18–19, 23
Middlesbrough, 55, 75
migrant groups, 37, 117, 134
Milan, 27, 83
Miner, H., 42
mining communities, 55, 89–90
Mohenjodaro, 20–21
monumental buildings: *see* buildings
Morocco, 14
Moscow, 28, 32
Moser, C. A., 92
motor cars, 32, 41, 63, 72, 99
movement, pattern of, 32, 97–99, 110–11
Mumford, L., 12, 25, 27, 56, 60, 72

Naples, 27, 83
Nash, John, 54
Nazirabad (*plan*), 41
Negroes, 124–7, 140
neighbourhoods, 64, 67–68, (*plan*) 68
Nelson, H. J., 91
neolithic revolution, 18–19, 22, 38
Nepal, 14
Netherlands, 6, 71–72, 84
new towns, 43, 52, 55, 64–69, 102, 112, 117
New York, 69, 70; age groups, 121; commuting, 110–11; concentric pattern, 140; density, 108; fertility ratio, 116; infantile mortality, 116; moving house, 111; Negroes, 125–7; segregation, (*maps*) 126; occupations and residential density, 122; population, 32, 33, 83; street pattern, 59; traffic, 62; water supply, 95
Newcastle, 100
newspapers, 11, 97, 100
Nigeria, 35, 39–41, 45, 112
Nile Valley, 19–21
'non-city', 60, 72
North America (*see also* United States): cities, 2, 38, 49; urbanization, 13–14, 33, 39, 48
Norway, 116
Norwich, 27, 80, 101

occupations, 89–92, 104–6, 109–10, 121–4; (*table*) 90; and class, 40, 121–4
Oceania, 13, 14
offices, 2, 41, 61–62, 74–75, 110
open spaces, 45, 49
Oslo, 116
Ottawa, 83
Oxford, 89–91, 101–2
Oyo, 39, (*plan*) 41

Pakistan, 14, 35–36
palaces, 28, 40, 48, 54, 138
Palermo, 28
Paris: growth, 45, 94; height of building limit, 75; infantile mortality, 116; influence, 81; population growth, 27, 28, 32; re-designed, 55
Park, R. E., 9
peasant communities, 17–19, 23–24, 35–37, 41, 50, 108
Peking, 46, 124, (*plan*) 47
Peru, 37, 50, 81–82
Petare, (*plan*) 47
Philadelphia, 32, 69
Pirenne, H., 4, 6–7, 10, 25, 27
Poor Law Institutions, 96; Unions, 96
population, capacity of big cities to absorb, 32–33, 111, 112; changes, 55, 111, 112; million cities, 2, 32–37; rural 13, 29; urban, 13–14, 16–17, 32–33 (*map*) 15; *see also* densities
prehistoric cities, 20–23
pre-industrial cities, 38–51, 77, 112–13, 117, 123, 129, 131, 136, 138
Priene, 59
'primate' cities (*see also* capital cities), 81, 83–84
Protestants, 119, 128, 131–3
Public Health Act (1848), 21
Puerto Ricans, 127
Pugin, Augustus, 58–59

racial differences, 124–7, 129

INDEX

railway stations, city, 58
railways, 30, 32, 60; elevated, 60, 62; underground, 60, 62
ranchos, 50–51
Rangoon, 112–13, 115, 129
rank-size rule, 83–84, 87
Rasmussen, S., 2
recreation land, 64, 69, 71
regional planning, 102; relationships, 10–11, 25, 80–81, 93–103; regions of influence, (*maps*) 98
religion, and origins of towns, 7
religious centres, 40; differences, 124–5, 130–3; and age groups, 119–20
renaissance cities, 27–28, 39, 49, 138
Rhondda Valleys, 55, 89–90
Rio de Janeiro, 49, 50
roads and streets, 20–21, 41, 44–46, 49, 52, 54, 56, 61; radial system, 23, 28, 70–72, 74; axial, 24, 26; focus of routes, 38, 46; *see also* grid system
Roman Catholics, 119, 128, 131–3
Roman towns, 24–26, 96
Rome, 24, 27, 82, 83
Rumania, 4, 16
rural districts, 96; population, 13, 14, 29, 37
Russia, 6, 14

Saigon, 2
St. Albans, 25, 26
St. Petersburg, 28, 32
San Francisco, 59
Scandinavia, 6, 31, 97
schools, 67, 71, 89, 97
Scotland, sex ratio, 114
Scott, W., 92
second-order cities (regions), 101–2
sector growth, 140–1
segregation of races, 124–7; based on religion, 130–3
services, 85, 87–89, 93–94, 97, 99–100, 105; functions of towns, 11, 75; carried underground, 66; industries, 75; distances travelled for, 87–89, 100
Seville, 27
sex ratio, 114–15, (*table*) 114; age groups, 118–21, 130

Shanghai, 44–45
shanty towns, 37, 50–51, 136–7
Sharon, 83
shire towns, 96
shopping facilities, 62–63, 68, 74, 75, 78; in centre of town, 38, 41, 43, 49, 62; with parking lot, 63; distances travelled for, 87–89, 100
Singapore, 72, 130
siting of cities, 10
size of towns and cities, 3–5, 8, 13, 32, 80–92; (*tables*), 82, 84, 85
Sjoberg, G., 39
skyscrapers, 26, 45, 59, 61–62, 71, 75, 139
slums, 43, 134–7, 141
Smailes, A. E., 11, 88, 97
social areas, 122–3, 140
society, differences between town and country, 8–9, 104–6, 113–34; rural, 104–6; technological stages, 39; urban, 11, 91–92, 96, 99, 104–6
South Africa, Union of, 14, 35
South America: *see* Latin America
South-East England, 2, 65, 94, 102, 112
Spain, 16, 23, 30, 81–82
spas, 28
specialist functions, areas and streets of, 76–78, (*map*) 76
specialization, 19, 20
Spengler, Oswald, 12
squares, 2, 28, 49, 54, 56, 60, 61
squatters: *see* shanty towns
Stalingrad, 71
standard of living, density and, 106–7
status: *see* class
streets: *see* roads and streets
suburbs, 2, 33, 42, 52, 60–62, 66, 72, 78, 139–40; residential, 3, 38, 49–50, 58, 139–40; density, 105, 107–10; age groups, 119–20
super-cities, 2, 30, 33
supermarkets, 49
Sweden, 3, 16, 30–31, 84
Switzerland, 16

tall buildings (*see also* skyscrapers), 45, 75
tank feature, 21

Taylor, G., 12
technical innovations, 28–29, 32, 59, 63
Tenochtitlan, 48
terraces, 52, 56, 58
theatres, 28, 74, 76, 88
third-order regions, 102
Tikal, 22
Timbuktu, 41–42, 46, 124
Tlaltelolco, 48
Tokyo, 32, 33, 116
town halls, 29, 58
towns, differences from cities, 4–5 (*see also* definitions); common elements, 38–40, 46, 47, 52
traffic in towns, 2, 62–63
tram-cars, 60
transition, zone of, 139, 140
transport, 60, 62, 96, 99, 108–9
Tregaron, 98–100
tributary areas, 85–86, (*table*) 86
trolley-buses, 60
Tuareg people, 42
Tunisia, 4, 14
Turkey, 4; size of towns, 83–84, (*table*) 84

Uganda, 14
'umland', 97
United Arab Republic (*see also* Egypt), 4, 14
United Kingdom: *see* Britain
United States of America: age groups, 117; central business districts, 74; classification of towns, 90, 91; definition of town, 3; density of cities, 108; ethnic groups, 127–9; fertility ratio, 116; garden cities, 66; industrialization, 29, 31, 59; infantile mortality, 116; megalopolis, 2, 12, 33, 69, 101; metropolitan cities, 33, 101; migrants, 31, 129, 134, 140; Negroes, 125–6, 140; size of cities, 83; urbanization, 14, 16, 31–32, 59; water supplies, 95
universities, 26, 89, 90
Unwin, Raymond, 65
urban districts, 96; population, 13, 14, 16, 17, 32–33, (*map*) 15; settlements, size and number (*table*), 13
'urban field', 97, 100
'urban revolution', 18, 22, 39
urbanization, process of, 13–37
USSR: *see* Russia
Utica, 127–9
Uxmal, 22

Valparaiso, 37
Van Thünen, 85
Venezuela: *barrios*, 50–51; cities, 37, (*plans*) 47; definition of town, 3; size of cities, 84, (*table*) 85; urbanization, 14, 16, 37
Verulamium, 24, 26
Victorian architecture, 58; building by-laws: *see under* houses and housing; cities and towns, 6, 66–67, 78, 133
Vidal de la Blache, P., 10
Vienna, 28, 32, 82; Zweig's description, 138
villages, 3, 5, 7, 17–20, 40; built behind terraces, 54

Wales: *bastide* towns, 26, 45, 49; influence of towns, 100, (*map*) 98; sex ratio, 114; shires, 96; water supply from mountains, 95
walls of towns and cities, 21–22, 24, 44–46, 53, 93, 131; function, 7–8, 25–26, 28, 40, 124
Walters Committee (1918), 66
Warsaw, 28
Washington, 69, 71, 84; age groups, 117; federal employees, 74, 75; planning of, 54–55; size 83
water supplies, 3, 94–95
way of life, urbanism as, 8–9
Welwyn Garden City, 66
West Africa, 34, 105, 123
Wirth, L., 8, 42, 106
Wren, Sir Christopher, 54
Wright, F. L., 70–71
Wycherley, R. E., 24

York, 27

ziggurats, 20, 22
Zipf, G. K., 83
zoning of industries, 21, 61, 65